Soul Walk

Before, During, and Afterlife

Cover and interior design by Sophia C. Russell
ISBN: 979-8-218-73239-4
Library of Congress Control Number: 2025918240
Printed in the United States of America
First Edition
Published by Prosperity House Publishing
https://prosperityhouse.co

This book is intended for informational and spiritual purposes only. It does not substitute professional advice or treatment. The author and publisher disclaim any liability arising from the use or misuse of this material. Readers are encouraged to use discernment and seek qualified guidance as needed.

References to biblical scriptures are included throughout this text. These references are intended for spiritual reflection, metaphysical exploration, and personal insight. The interpretations presented herein are the author's own and do not represent the views of any religious organization or denomination. Readers are encouraged to approach the material with an open mind and apply discernment in alignment with their own spiritual beliefs and experiences.

This book includes general background information on the topic of channeling as part of a broader spiritual discussion. It is intended for informational and reflective purposes only and is not a how-to manual or instructional resource for practicing channeling or any related metaphysical techniques.

Prosperity House Publishing is a Black woman-owned independent press dedicated to amplifying spiritual, holistic, and metaphysical voices from diverse communities.

For permissions or bulk purchase inquiries, please contact:

The Prosperity House
Dallas, Texas, USA
prosperityhouse.co
help.prosperity@gmail.com
469-868-6061

Soul Walk

Before, During, and Afterlife

A transformative journey into the heart of
true spiritual awakening

SOPHIA C. RUSSELL

Prosperity House Publishing

Dedication

To the seekers, the dreamers, the healers, and those who remember. May your hearts be healed with love, and your souls walk free.

Table of Contents

SOPHIA C. RUSSELL

Preface

Soul Walk was written for anyone who has ever felt the quiet tug that there might be more to your own soul but felt too afraid to explore it. Maybe you were raised in a religion that gave you structure, a sense of belonging, and a foundation for your beliefs. But somewhere along the way, you began to wonder if you have the whole story. If this is you, I want you to know that you are not alone.

We live in a world that teaches us early on to thoughtlessly trust outside authority, whether it's through family, church, culture, or society at large. So many of us were shaped by messages about who God is, what's acceptable to believe, and what happens if we dare to ask questions. Little by little, we learn to doubt ourselves instead of listening to the divine voice already whispering within us.

The truth is, you have always had access to divine wisdom, not through someone else, but within yourself. This book is not here to tell you what to believe. It's here to remind you that you already carry the connection you are looking for. All that's needed is practice, the practice of trusting your intuition, recognizing your inner guidance, and reclaiming your spiritual free will.

As I stepped into this new sense of freedom, fear showed up at every turn. Still, I pressed forward—and my greatest ally was reading. Once I discovered the first book that truly spoke to me (which I'll share more about), it opened a floodgate to many others, each one deepening my understanding and I devoured them with hunger. But whenever someone asked me about my journey or sought guidance, I found myself pointing them to many of those same books.

Over time however, I realized a pattern. In some cases, the person didn't connect with the material I recommended, or they'd come back to me and ask, "Do you have a book?" Each time I was asked that question I felt a sting, because though I couldn't get pen to paper quite yet, Soul Walk had already been stirring inside of me.

As I considered what information to discuss, I felt called to weave together the insights I was gathering, from many teachers, sacred texts, and my own lived experiences into one cohesive body of work. Soul Walk is the result: a blend of metaphysical wisdom, mental health awareness, spiritual insight, religious education, and practical tools designed to help you navigate your own path with clarity. Oddly, this was not as difficult as I thought, as you will see in reading, all of these concepts are already uniquely intertwined.

The journey of human life while communal is at the same time very personal, and sometimes it's scary to step away from what's familiar. Thus I created this book to support you as you begin to remember who you truly are, not who you were told to be.

I invite you to take each step gently, with openness and curiosity. My writing, if it does what I intend, should challenge you to grow and provide support to aid in your upliftment. As you read please remember, you are not walking away from God; you are walking toward the truth that has always been within you.

1 The Bridge to Remembering

"Your soul is not something that you have, it is who you are. Despite what you have been taught, your soul can never be sold or taken, and it does not need to be saved because it can never be lost."—Seth Speaks, 1972

Soul Walk is for those on a quest, seeking answers, clarity, and a way to define their own truth. This book does not aim to diminish or judge religion, individual life paths, personal beliefs about God, the origins of humanity, creation, science, or philosophy. Instead, its purpose is to provide a clearer, deeper understanding of all of these.

Along with references from various sources, I also use biblical passages throughout this text. Not because I believe the Bible is the only way to learn about God, but because I think there are many, like me, who were also taught that the Bible is the *only* word of God. I also found that there are many people who have realized that there is more to learn beyond what is traditionally taught in our churches but may be hesitant or fearful to explore.

As I teach, I will highlight how scripture supports the information I share. For instance, in 2 Corinthians, Paul mentions giving the people milk instead of solid food because they were behaving like spiritual infants. Much of the teaching in his letters represents this "milk." However, the time has come for humanity to transition to solid food, deeper spiritual truths. Think of this book as a bridge between milk and solid food,

1

sort of like the Gerber baby food we give the child as the digestive system develops.

When I first started to learn and study the information I am presenting here, I was both perplexed and excited and as stated, a little scared. I had spent much of my life being miseducated by society and by well-intentioned caregivers, churches, and schools. It's no wonder I felt sad and unsettled most of the time, these are the feelings that come with extended periods of confusion. This miseducation and confusion are something millions of people experience, and as a result individually and collectively it brings chaos. Just look around you.

Discovering this ancient wisdom was like tasting the richest, most nourishing meal of my life and I couldn't get enough. The deeper I studied, the more questions arose. At first, my mind struggled to grasp it all, overwhelmed and uncertain. But as I pressed on, the pieces began to fit, and the truth revealed itself with stunning clarity. Through this book, I hope to offer fellow seekers, those yearning for something deeper than religion, a thoughtful and expansive guide, rich enough to ignite your own awakening.

About This Book

Though the subtitle, "Before, During, and After Life," gives the impression of a linear expression of time and living, they are not. Time and living are multidimensional and multifaceted experiences where past, present, and future (before, during, and after) are all happening at the same time, in the precious *Present Moment*.

For example, I live in Texas which is in the Central Time Zone. Let's say at noon I call my sister in California, the Pacific Time Zone, it is 10 am there. You could say, from my perspective, that I have called into the past. As we are chatting on the phone, we wonder how our cousin is doing in New York (Eastern time) where it is 1pm. From our perspective we have called the future, but in truth we are all chatting in the same present moment. If we were to call a friend in China, which is 14 hours ahead of me, and 16 hours ahead of California, we'd be calling into tomorrow, but it is still the same present moment, it is just that each of our individual perspectives of that moment vary.

It is likely that at this point in your life, you are living according to a particular set of core beliefs and what I have said so far is producing some kind of reaction in you. Perhaps curiosity, confusion, or maybe even a little judgment. All of these are natural; I suggest you go to a quiet place and ask yourself if this is something you should continue reading, then wait patiently for the answer, it can come in any number of ways. When you have decided to continue reading, it is important to be open, not being so quick to shut down knowledge unfamiliar to you because of the beliefs and traditions that were handed down to you by those who, through love, thought they were teaching you correctly.

In this book, we'll explore the origins and purpose of the Bible, along with alternative paths to understanding and experiencing God. Together, we'll examine who (or what) God is and is not, the nature of human consciousness, the soul, and the creation of the universe and everything within it. We'll also dive into questions about where we come from before birth, how we design our life journeys, and what happens after we leave this world. Additionally, I'll touch on the evolution of humanity and our unique role on Earth.

This is a lot of material, so as we move along, I will often shift topics a bit just to give some necessary background information before moving forward. You may also find that I repeat certain concepts throughout, this was purposely done so that you gain more in depth understanding of the information. Much of this knowledge predates scripture, so I have also included references and a glossary of suggested teachers in the back of the book. *Let's go.*

2 More Than This Life

Ever since I can remember I have wanted to know more about where I came from. How I got here, to Earth, in a body. More about life, creation, who God is, and how the beginning began. I remember being a very little girl and knowing that there was something greater and bigger, that there was more to life than this one simple existence we call a lifetime.

My parents were not religious, and our family didn't go to church with any regularity. I remember a few sparse instances of my mother taking us with a friend, occasionally we'd go for a funeral or wedding, or I'd ask to go with a neighbor. But I wouldn't say there was much discussion in our home about God at all. Despite this, I have always had this inner knowing that there is more to who I am than what my eyes could see, and I felt compelled to figure it out.

I'd just look into the sky sometimes and ponder what was out there beyond what is visible. I wondered about the planets, what they were like, and if there were people there. I never doubted that there could be, but were they like us? Even as a child, I remember thinking it was strange that humanity does not acknowledge the probability of intelligent life on other planets, even teaching definitively in schools that there is not.

Though our modern scientific practices are still very limited, it has been estimated that there is one planet per star, this means there are more than 2 trillion planets. I said TRILLION, not million, not billion. We proclaim that our Creator is limitless and that all things are possible with God. Yet in the same breath, we impose our own limitations on the Creator, assuming that intelligent life exists only on one small planet in a universe of trillions. In doing so, we confine God's infinite creativity to the narrow bounds of our beliefs.

Consider this, each human body is like a universe in itself. Just like the cosmos we each carry about 30 trillion blood cells at any given time. Now imagine the size of one single blood cell within your physical body (a pin dot) and it being the only one with oxygen in it. Ridiculous right? Believing that humans on Earth are alone in the universe is a lot like this.

But what does my life, my soul, and God have to do with the cosmos, celestial life, and the Universe? How do these pieces fit together?

In the churches I attended, these concepts were never discussed. As I studied my Bible however, my desire to understand more only got stronger, and I began boldly exploring the vastness of who God truly is. I say boldly because, without fully realizing it, I had been deeply conditioned by a societal belief system I mistakenly thought I had chosen through free will.

Many of us assume we are born into our religion or faith or that we consciously choose it, often without realizing how deeply our faith is shaped or sometimes inherited, by the culture surrounding us. Rather than a personal spiritual discovery, our beliefs are frequently absorbed from societal norms, family traditions, and national identity, making it difficult to separate genuine conviction from cultural conditioning.

Having been a devout Christian since my baptism at the age of 18, it wasn't until I was in my 30's that I felt a profound shift. Something deep within me awakened, a yearning I could no longer ignore. I began to see through society's façade and realized I had to take an active role in discovering truth for myself.

I had studied the scriptures and asked questions all throughout my Christian walk. Some of them were answered, but many were not, and this left my mind unsettled. And if you are a Christian like I was, you'd probably be sure that all the answers lie in the Bible and in the man we call Jesus, because without a doubt I believed that too.

However, in trying not to grow bitter and even more confused, I prayed for answers. And yes, answers did come. But what my higher guidance led me to read was not my Bible, which I had spent over 20 years studying daily and loved very much. However, I had to admit, through this time of spiritual questioning, I was not getting what I needed from the scriptures or from my church community.

After a morning prayer and quiet time pondering my inner turmoil. I picked up my Bible and prayed to be directed to something that would help me. Then I flipped through and attempted to read a few different passages, but nothing I read was really helping me like it once had. So I closed my eyes, took a deep breath and said, "Lord, I know you are always with me."

When I opened my eyes, I felt compelled to get up and look out onto my husband's bookshelf. There nestled between 100 or more colorless book covers on the shelves, was a bright yellow book almost glowing at me. The spine read "Esoteric Encyclopedia of Eternal Knowledge." I am still a bit ashamed to admit that at that time, I did not know what *esoteric* meant and don't think I had ever heard the word before.

Let me just add here, throughout my life, I had believed that I did not enjoy reading. In fact, aside from the Bible, I had never finished an entire book. I must have been about 30 years old when I finally picked up a novel on my own, read it cover to cover in just a few days, and absolutely loved it. That's when I realized it wasn't reading I disliked; it was the books that had been assigned to me in school that I didn't resonate with.

Anyway, I asked my husband what the word esoteric meant, and the natural teacher that he is, he replied, "You should look it up." So I did, and I read the book cover to cover. Studying it, going back and forth through it, highlighting and pondering the knowledge departed in it. What a wonderful piece of literature.

From then on answers began to unfold. Now I am sharing some of this knowledge with you. Not because I have stopped learning, as learning never stops, but because I know what I have to share is actually useful in living a happier more fulfilled life. Even though my higher guidance didn't lead me back to my Bible or the man we call Jesus, it most assuredly led me to understand them like I had never before.

Now I know what was meant by the passage in John 4 "but whoever drinks the water I give them will never thirst. Indeed, the water I give them will become in them a spring of water welling up to eternal life."

3 Reflection: Awakening to the Inner Mind

"Truly I tell you, unless you change and become like little children, you will never enter the kingdom of heaven."
—*Matthew 18:3*

When I was a young girl, I remember riding in the back seat of the family car on long drives. Sometimes, I'd gaze out of the window looking at all the other vehicles, the streets, and the hustle and bustle of the city. Then as the road changed and we'd shift out onto the long two-lane highway going through farmland and barren fields, I'd suddenly find myself looking through what seemed to be someone else's eyes. It's hard to describe really, it was like I was in a daze and part of my consciousness was in another place.

During these times I might suddenly find myself sitting in bleachers watching a football game or walking around a park with others. I would not describe these "visions" as dreams because I was not asleep, nor "daydreaming" in the typical since of the word, because usually in daydreams you initiate thinking about something or someone, say a love interest. Then you commence to imagine being out with them, what you'd do, etc.

In my case, these "visions" just appear out of my conscious control, and I'm there, involved in another life so to speak. I say looking through someone else's eyes because sometimes I can see the frame around the inside of their eyes, sort of like looking through the frames of glasses. It's still hard to really describe. I just know that a part of me is literally somewhere else.

9

As I got older, the visions became fewer and farther between. Instead of happening while on long drives it would happen mostly when I was just waking up from sleep, and it is very different from a dream while sleeping. Occasionally I can just close my eyes and have them briefly.

I never thought of these occurrences as strange or odd, they were normal to me. Honestly, I thought they were something everyone experienced, until I mentioned it to others on a few occasions, and no one knew what I was talking about. When I realized I was the only one having this experience, I tried to dismiss it, but the visions were too vivid to ignore.

A few days after having a vision I typically forget about it. I can't say that they are premonitions, as I've never seen anyone I recognize from my current life and usually, the person is involved in mundane ordinary tasks, nothing very exciting. But there are times when I come out of them very moved. Particularly, there was one when suddenly I was in a young man who had just robbed a small neighborhood market.

I entered his head just as he was tearing out of the store and running down the street. To my shock, he was shooting a gun back at the person chasing him. Somehow, I knew that he had just robbed the store and that it was the owner running after him, even though I wasn't with him for that part. I had the feeling I was in New York sometime in the 1980's, though when I had the vision it was 2016.

As he ran through the streets looking back over his shoulder, he was scared and worried and I felt his fear. It was more intense than any fear I had ever felt as Sophia. He was thinking of his family, a young son to be exact, and afraid to die. His heart was beating rapidly, and I felt a strong need to calm him down. So, telepathically I communicated with him, saying, "it's ok, you'll be ok. It will work out, you won't die."

I wanted desperately to stay with him, but alas my focus of attention forced me back to this reality and I left him. As I was returning, the streets of the city faded. Then like a swoosh, I was fully back, and I laid there bewildered wondering, "What the heck was that?" In my waking state I do not know telepathy, but because of these visions I understand it, and have experienced it often.

As strange as my little story sounds, it happens and it's difficult to dismiss it as a dream because it is a very real experience, the only thing is that physically I am not there. I realize this sounds like some kind of sci fi quantum leap or a "That's So Raven" episode, and I'm convinced that many screenwriters and filmmakers are more informed about alternate realities than we give them credit for. Even quantum physics supports the idea that the human consciousness is far more multidimensional than we currently comprehend.

Sidebar: The Other 90%

We've all heard that we only use about 10% of our brain's potential. That idea has always made me wonder: What's going on with the other 90%?

While neuroscientists have clarified that we do use all parts of the brain to physically function, the idea points to a deeper truth: we're only using about 10% of our full human potential.

Psychologist William James once said, "We are making use of only a small part of our possible mental and physical resources." He wasn't talking about neurons—he was talking about consciousness, creativity, intuition, and spiritual power. We live much of our lives on autopilot, shaped by routine, culture, and survival needs, while much greater inner capacities lie dormant.

What if someone, even unknowingly, began tapping into just 1% more than the norm? What might we begin to see, feel, or understand that usually stays hidden? Could it be that the visions, insights, or "downloads" some of us experience aren't strange at all, but simply glimpses of what becomes available when the mind opens just a bit wider?

Late in 2014 is when I'll designate the time that I started to "wake up" and understand more about the laws of the universe. Sadly, before that time the only universal law I knew about was gravity. And I think there are too many people who don't know that there are other important laws governing our universe that impact us individually and collectively. I often heard the phrase "God is law" but still my understanding of that was limited.

In reflection, I see now that all my life experiences, the good, bad, and the ugly were needed for me to be who and where I am now. I never liked it when I heard people say that, and here I am saying it. I didn't like it, because I had been through some very hard things and had not yet understood the purpose of having those experiences.

I had been taught to "love your neighbor as yourself" which I strove to do, however this scripture is often taught with the focus on loving your *neighbor* not loving *yourself.* Upon self-examining I realized that I didn't love myself, so how could I love another? And greater still if I don't love myself, how could I love God?

The odd thing is, I did not know I didn't love myself; I had never even considered what that meant, but when I did start to think about it, I knew I didn't. At this point I began to pay more attention to myself, my habits, and inner thoughts. The subtle thoughts that sneak in. You can hear them most when you're driving, cooking, cleaning, or doing something routine.

The truth is, we are narrating life in our minds every moment. From the time we open our eyes in the morning, to the time we fall into deep sleep there is a constant mental narrative. When I intentionally paid close attention to that narration, or "mental chatter" as I have learned to call it, it was eye opening to say the least.

Most of my thoughts around my relationships, money, career, goals, almost everything I found were doubtful, worrisome, or confusing. And it wasn't until I started tuning into them that I found out how many of my thoughts provoked anxiety and grief. I realized that underneath everything, my baseline mood was sad, and I didn't know the origin of my sadness. When I thought back through my lived experiences, I felt it started somewhere in my teens, but it was difficult for me to pinpoint when it began. Of course I had pockets of happiness, but these were fleeting and were usually dependent upon some life event or circumstance that turned out well.

However, this was not the Sophia people saw. If you were to ask someone who knew me during that time, I'm confident they would tell you they are surprised by my confession. After all, when I discovered it, I myself was surprised. Going through each day doing what needed to be done, I hadn't done much self-reflection or given my inner world much attention, and I didn't conduct myself like someone depressed or sad. To me, I was just living my life and rolling with the punches. I had unintentionally created a facade that I began to live behind so that I appeared ok to others.

In truth, I had difficulty looking in the mirror. I zeroed in on any and every flaw, did what I could to fix myself up, but then I walked away feeling ugly. I disliked the sound of my voice and my overall disposition. As a young wife and mother, I was unprepared, insecure, impatient, and quick tempered. At times, I was rude and very critical of others. I ruminated over my mistakes and failures, feeling regretful a lot of the time. If I received a promotion or if someone congratulated me on an achievement, I thanked them gratefully, but really, I figured they were just being polite or that I got the promotion by default. I always excused my accomplishments as a one off, or easy, saying to myself that anyone could do it. There was nothing special about me and no room to esteem myself.

I am reminded of a scripture where Paul in discussing marriage said, "For no one ever hated his own flesh, but he nourishes and cherishes it, just as Christ does the church (Ephesians 5:29)." In teaching men how to love their wives, Paul assumed that the husband already loved himself and directs him to love his wife as he loves himself.

While this passage may be a guide for many, look around you, there is an innumerable amount of people who hate their own flesh, I was one of them. And when you enter a marriage without this understanding, then try to love someone else without realizing that you do not love yourself, things can get bad quickly. As a therapist, I often ask clients early in therapy, "Do you love yourself?" First comes silence, then the answer I would say about 8 out of 10 times is, No.

I learned through these times of self-examining that there are two paths of thought going on in my mind, and yet another part listening and choosing. One path of thought seemed to be sort of chattering about everything, trying to figure things out, and another part of my mind noticed the chatter. This part seemed calmer and wiser while unintrusive. Then there is what seems to be *me,* who could choose between the two. In noticing this sort of separation (or different streams of thought) I realized that the one I chose to follow or believe, had a significant impact on my emotions, behavior, and experiences with others.

Navigating the Landscape of the Mind

I call the calmer corrective path of thought my *higher mind* or sometimes (*higher/inner guidance*). Which I feel is the part of me that is still *non-physical* (where I was before becoming physical). And the other chattering part, the *ego mind*. This is the mind that is given to us to conduct ourselves here on Earth as humans. It is equipped to help us learn, remember, analyze and learn basic abilities such as walking, talking, activities, names, responsibilities and so on.

The ego mind tends to be worrisome, insecure, negative, and dramatic. It loves attention and immediate gratification, and it needs to be disciplined. We connect with the ego mind as if it is who we are and identify all of the thoughts it produces as true, when many of them are not. The ego mind should be treated as a tool, like our limbs. If your feet were to just start walking you around the room, you would immediately make attempts to correct it. However, we let our minds run around like a toddler in Walmart with no guidance or direction.

The higher mind helps us to navigate the more complex parts of our experiences like self-discipline, relationships, tough decisions, maintaining peace, etc. However, most of us don't readily know about these varying parts of our mind, and not only do we believe in the chaotic chatter of the ego mind, but we do not even learn to rely on and exercise the expertise of the higher mind. Constantly dismissing it, and then saying things like, "Something told me not to do that, and I didn't listen." Some of us have silenced the higher mind so many times that it has become faint and distant, while the ego mind,

15

the clanging symbol that it is, has our full attention. As the saying goes, *attention is currency, invest it wisely.*

We must be purposeful about where our attention is focused as we will certainly live out what we are focused upon. This is the meaning to passages like "you reap what you sow." Our thoughts are seeds being planted into the subconscious, and those seeds will grow into whatever fruit is planted. If I am consistently focusing my attention on the lack of things, like love or money, lack in these areas will be amplified in my day-to-day experiences.

After these varying parts of the mind were revealed to me, I still had and still have work to do. I started by monitoring my thoughts and mental chatter more closely. This practice helped me to catch and challenge those thoughts the ego mind throws out constantly as it is trying to assist in figuring things out. The goal is to exercise utilizing the higher mind as much as possible instead. As you do this the connection becomes stronger over time.

The ego mind does not know what to do in more emotional and complex problems, so it goes to the past (what happened before) or to the future (what may happen) and it tends to lean towards the negative leaving us feeling like the positive possibilities are unlikely. When in actuality a positive outcome is equally as likely. The deciding factor is YOU and where you choose to focus your attention.

These negative streams of thought become like bright, shiny lures, getting our full attention, while other possible truths go unnoticed, so they rarely manifest. Many individuals use all their energy equating being *realistic* with the negative in effort to avoid being hurt or disappointed. We remain unaware of our own power to produce the preferred outcome and seem to be silently awaiting help from some source outside of ourselves. This mode of thinking leaves us feeling anxious and depressed.

Through training myself to recognize these parts of my mind, I have come a long way in handling difficulty. For example, I used to have anxiety and panic attacks, before I even knew what they were. On a couple of occasions, it was so bad that I went to the emergency room feeling as though I was having a heart attack.

Through monitoring my thoughts, I have learned that I can choose the ones that align with my goals to create a narrative that feels better. When anxiety arises today, I can typically calm it quickly. Bear in mind this is a practice that takes time and will vary from person to person. Having someone to assist you like a therapist who is trained in Cognitive Behavior Therapy, Solution Focused Therapy, or Narrative methods of therapy can be useful, but it is not necessary.

"Finally, brothers and sisters, whatever is true, whatever is noble, whatever is right, whatever is pure, whatever is lovely, whatever is admirable, if anything is excellent or praiseworthy, **think** about such things (Philippians 4:8)."

The writer of the scripture is not telling us to *act* holier but gives us a practical approach to managing our thoughts. When we have the understanding that our thoughts are powerful, and are creating our lived experience, we can learn to detach from the negative and choose better thoughts.

As we embark on this journey of self-awareness, it is essential to understand that the process of transformation is not immediate. Change takes time, and it requires a consistent intentional practice of choosing better thoughts, challenging old patterns, and tuning into the wisdom of the higher mind.

We can learn to release the grip of the ego mind and make space for the peace and clarity that comes from aligning with the God mind. It is a commitment to investing in our inner world, and the reward is a life that reflects our truest potential, a life that feels more intentional, balanced, and free.

You are the architect of your own experience, and it begins with the power of the thoughts you choose to believe. With patience and persistence, you can begin to rewrite the narrative of your life.

Sidebar: Meeting My Higher Self

One night, while my body rested in sleep, my consciousness traveled to another dimension (whether you realize it or not, yours does too). In that realm, I encountered the most awe-inspiring feminine presence I had ever witnessed.

She stood about five to eight feet away from me, radiant and breathtaking, yet her beauty transcended anything physical. It wasn't the kind of beauty we recognize in a traditionally attractive woman; it was something vastly different, a deeply majestic and regal state of being.

Her spirit was confident, unapologetic, and bold. While peace, acceptance, security, and safety emanated from her. It was very overwhelming. Her frequency was so high that I could not move any closer, and though I attempted a few times, I had difficulty looking directly at her.

Her form was human-like, but her body was an illuminating but soft, golden light. Not merely glowing from her, but she seemed to be composed of the light itself. In awe I remained silent, suspended in wonder and reverence.

*When I finally found the courage to speak, mystified I asked, "Who **are** you?" she replied with quiet grace, "I am* *you." Immediately I wept. In that moment, I could not compre-hend how something so divine, so radiant, so indescribably magnificent, could possibly be me.*

SOPHIA C. RUSSELL

4 The Transmission of Wisdom Beyond Scripture

"Her officials within her are like wolves tearing their prey; they shed blood and kill people to make unjust gain. Her prophets whitewash these deeds for them by false visions and lying divinations. They say, 'This is what the Sovereign Lord says'—when the Lord has not spoken. The people of the land practice extortion and commit robbery; they oppress the poor and needy and mistreat the foreigner, denying them justice."
—*Ezekiel 22:27-29*

While many aspects of our society have advanced dramatically over the past century, it's perplexing how medical and space research seem to have stagnated when compared with the developments in technology. Despite the trillions of dollars poured annually into these disciplines, the realization is that significant breakthroughs are lacking.

In medical science, the trillions of dollars generated and reinvested yearly mostly result in more pharmaceuticals that mask symptoms rather than offer cures. Similarly, our space programs appear to have stalled since the early 1970's. If we did in fact land on the moon, why haven't we returned since 1972? That's over 50 years.

We are told that returning to the Moon, or going beyond it, is prohibitively expensive, requires immense resources, and demands cutting-edge technology. But let's not forget that over 5 decades ago, the Apollo 11 mission reportedly achieved a manned Moon landing with far less technological sophistication than we have today.

That mission took about a decade of preparation, cost approximately $355 million, and involved a coordinated effort

21

of around 400,000 people spanning government, corporate, and scientific sectors. Given that foundation, shouldn't we be far more advanced by now? The lack of progress doesn't quite make sense, and the official explanations feel increasingly thin. So the real question becomes: What aren't we being told?

Collectively we place not only our hard earned money, but also immense trust in our world governments and leaders, believing they are operating in our best interest. As we focus on our daily lives, we rely on these officials to handle the complex issues of research and societal advancement. Some might argue that calling them "gods" is an exaggeration, but it reflects how they create and enforce laws that we must follow, often under threat of punishment.

While I'm not against government, I believe we are witnessing a troubling imbalance of power, with authorities intruding into areas that should be between individuals and their own beliefs.

While we give our leaders the respect of gods, who or what is that all encompassing guiding force we refer to as God?

Throughout history God has been given many names. For the sake of this reading, I will also call God *Source* or *All That Is*. By this I mean the original beginning of everything, to include all possibilities and probabilities. This Creator Source is *"All That There Is."* Not just the beginning of Earth and humans, but everything, the entirety of the cosmos and all within it.

Because of how we (as humans) learn and how we teach, people throughout time, in trying to explain the unexplainable and describe the indescribable, have used allegories, parables, metaphors, stories, and symbols and have conveyed these in various languages to define God and describe our creation. As generatiopass;ss, these stories and the information are translated into other languages and edited over and over and over again.

Among the many problematic issues involved in translating and editing repeatedly is that in the process, some of the true meaning is lost. In some cases, those translating and interpreting have confused Earth's beginning with the beginning of all things. They have confused or blended Source with other governing beings, creators who came out of the Source and called them God. Additionally, they have credited or charged our Source with the actions of those other beings.

Concepts such as cursing and blessing, for example are attributed to God, when our Source allows free will learning and growth. If you take a moment to reflect, often times what we think is a blessing or a curse initially, turns out to be the opposite.

When I was a Christian and asked about this, I was told simply that despite translation, God is able to keep his word in order. So I think it's important to look at this concept of "keeping his word in order" a little deeper. It is good for me to note here, the practices of hermeneutics, epistemology, and etymology.

In short these are the practices used in interpretation of texts, to translate languages, to differentiate between facts, beliefs, and opinions. To understand the use of words, how they are used within various cultures, and how that use changes throughout time. Those who are responsible for translating, particularly ancient texts to include Biblical scriptures, use these methods in hopes of conveying the most accurate translation possible. But do they?

23

When I was very young the word "gay" was taking a transition. There were still texts and television shows that used it to describe one who is happy and joyful. Today however, I have a son in his preteens, if he came into the house smiling and laughing and I were to ask him, "Son, why are you so gay?" He would for sure be taken aback. He may even wonder why I think his happiness means that he is homosexual. This word has completed its transition into an entirely different meaning, and there will come a time, say a hundred years from now, where the majority of people do not know that to be gay once meant to be joyful and had nothing to do with sexual orientation.

Maybe you have played the game "Telephone." This is a game wherein a group of people sit in a circle, usually about 5 or more. The first person thinks of a short random phrase, such as, *"When I was 6, I loved pancakes and jumping rope."* Then they whisper it into the ear of the person seated next to them, then that person whispers it to the person next to them, and so on.

What happens when the phrase gets back to the original person? It has now become, *"I ate 6 pancakes for breakfast and tripped over a rope."* When the first person repeats the original phrase aloud, everyone falls out in laughter. Here we have a small example of how people easily change entire structures of sentences in one language, in one small group, and in only minutes. Yet when it comes to the translation of ancient texts, which have gone through a series of interpretations and languages over thousands of years, we expect that these common human errors did not happen.

It is a real possibility that someone researching our current library of texts **2000** years from now could miss something about how we use words today. Especially since we use words like, "bad, sick, and dope," to also mean "awesome." Let's say the etymologist was very thorough in researching back from the year 4030 to 2030, confident in their interpretation of the word gay to mean homosexual.

They state how assured they are in their translation because their research covers a span of 2000 years. However, the text they interpreted was initially written around 1930. After all, what's a hundred years when you've gone through 2000 years of information?

Now, someone new comes along and challenges the old fellow on his translation, but all the research has been done, reviewed, approved by the peers of the original translator, and printed up. The new guy doesn't get much support, except from maybe those few who do not follow along with the mainstream teaching.

Similar scenarios often happen in real life. For example, The Sphinx and pyramids at Giza. Hundreds of years ago, both were given approximate ages and uses, and the agreement was made to type up what was theorized by those researchers and teach it to the masses. After all these huge anomalies had to be explained to the public somehow.

Today, most of what was theorized has been disproved. Such as the teaching that the pyramids are tombs, yet a mummy has never been recovered inside of them. And when comparing the pyramids to the actual tombs of the pharaohs found in the Valley of the Kings, there are no similarities.[1] [2]

Over the years reputable investigators such as engineer and author Christopher Dunn have found physical evidence that challenge the Great Pyramid at Giza as a tomb, showing

---

[1] Lehner, *The Complete Pyramids* (1997).
[2] Reeves and Wilkinson, *The Complete Valley of the Kings* (1996).

strong scientific support for its use as a power plant[3]. Another is Dr. Robert Schoch, a graduate of Yale University, who holds degrees in anthropology, geology, and geophysics.

When Dr. Schoch and his team released scientific evidence that supported his water erosion hypothesis, which redated the Sphinx to over 11,000 years ago[4], his research was shunned by both the mainstream scientific and archeological communities. Each of these reputable researchers are ignored by mainstream academia and their findings are called "fringe claims."

Additionally, while in the research field Dr. Schoch stumbled upon previously unknown chambers within and underneath the Sphinx. Schoch, along with other researchers, have speculated that these chambers might contain artifacts or historical evidence that could shed light on the origins of the Sphinx and its purpose.

However, these discoveries remain unverified. Once they were reported, the Egyptian government shut down Schoch's research and no excavation has been allowed to confirm the exact nature of these anomalies, and the chambers remain unexplored. Our contemporary governments are not prepared to acknowledge that these ancient civilizations possessed electrical power and were likely more technologically advanced than we are today.

As a young woman it had always been my understanding that varying fields of research were set in place so that as discoveries are made, we would update our current record of history, allowing a more thorough understanding of it. However, as physical evidence emerges that should rewrite the

---

[3] Dunn. *The Giza Power Plant: Technologies of Ancient Egypt.* (1998).

[4] Schoch, *Redating the Great Sphinx of Giza.* (1992).

textbooks, it seems to get hidden, ignored, or debunked rather than explored.

Not to beat a dead horse but I think this might be another ideal example. Let's take the word *love*. In English we use this one word no matter what we are talking about. I love my family, I love Mexican food, I love my comfy sweats, I love reading, I love old school R&B, I love the smell of fresh flowers, and I love God.

Surely if someone asked me to choose between these that would be an absurd request. Fluent English speakers just know these are distinct kinds of love. In other languages, however, there are different words to express these distinctions. But when you translate from them to English you only have the one word, *love;* so we may not have the best understanding of what the original text meant.

In ancient Greek, for example, there were 4 different words for love. This is the language in which a highly misunderstood scripture is written, 1 Timothy 6:10 "For the love of money is the root of all evil." The original Greek word used for love here was *philargyria*. This word is better translated as avarice, meaning *greed for money with a reluctance to share or give*.

Now I am not an etymologist, but you can see how easy it is even for the most well-trained translator to choose the word that he/she thinks fits best, and mis-educate thousands upon thousands of people who will never know anything about the original text. So now if I were to say, "greed for money is the root of evil." Then you have another understanding of the passage all together.

Along with all the other things I love, and since there is only the one word in English, I'd have to say that I love money.

I love it when my bills are due, when my kids need things, when it's time to get groceries, when I want to buy myself something nice, and I love it when someone pays me what I am worth for the work that I do.

Throughout my life, there have been many times when I needed to handle important responsibilities like these but had no money to do so. Yet somehow, I found a way. And each time I did, especially when I was able to pay off a debt, I didn't feel pride or greed, but a deep sense of appreciation. Those moments taught me the value of faith, resourcefulness, and trust in divine timing. In contrast, when a person becomes consumed by the pursuit of money, driven by greed or desperation rather than purpose, it often leads to suffering for themselves and for others.

Some might say, "Of course that's what it means, I already knew that." However, I emphasize this distinction because our individual relationship with money varies from person to person. Someone who grew up in abundance, never experiencing lack, will interpret this scripture differently than someone who has lived with financial struggle. In my experience, it is those living in these extremes who have been most impacted by the misunderstanding of this passage.

Wherever you find yourself on the spectrum between poverty and wealth, tune in to your thoughts around money. The wealthy person may feel guilty or bad about their wealth. Going through painstaking lengths to sacrifice and prove they love God or others, more than their money, when they were never greedy in the first place. The person living in poverty feels guilty for wanting more, thinking that somehow their desire means that they are ungrateful or compromises their love for the Creator, which it does not in any way. Now, the feeling of guilt carries a low *frequency* and when felt for extended periods can lead to many other problems. (We will discuss frequency more later in the book).

Calling God "father" is another word that has given us many ideas about who or what Source is. And the beliefs, thoughts, and images this example conjures are just as varied as there are creatures on the Earth. It is likely these teachers were using their experience *with* a father to describe an aspect of what God is *like*, not who or what God actually *is*. God is All, if you are a Bible reader you know there are numerous scriptures which say so. Here are just a few.

Hebrews 2:10 "In bringing many sons and daughters to glory, it was fitting that God, for whom and through whom everything exists....."

Colossians 1:16 "For by him all things were created, in heaven and on earth, visible and invisible, whether thrones or dominions or rulers or authorities, all things were created through him and for him."

John 1:3 "Through him all things were made; without him nothing was made that has been made."

Though the writer refers to our Source in the masculine, these passages convey that God is everything. Both mother and father, feminine and masculine, not one or the other. And at the same time God our Source is neither because these are human concepts used to describe characteristics in physical terms.

Referring to the Source of everything as a *he*, likely came about because masculinity or the male is often depicted as the "protector" and "provider." However, because the rigid gender roles our society perpetuates heavily influence our thinking, we may miss the fact that females also protect and provide.

29

Additionally, we attribute masculine and feminine characteristics to match biological sex, and we should not. Every human embryo begins undifferentiated (the same) and will follow female development by default unless testosterone (via the *SRY* gene) directs male development. Thus, all men and women innately have both feminine and masculine qualities which vary in their expression from person to person. Our fabricated gender norms make life difficult for men who are natural nurturers and care givers and women who may not be. I make this a point here for the realization that the Source is everything, All That Is, not *just* a he.

"Does the rain have a father? Who fathers the drops of dew? From whose womb comes the ice? Who gives birth to the frost from the heavens when the waters become hard as stone? (Job 38: 28-30)." Here the writer discusses God in both the masculine (father) and the feminine (birth & womb). If God did not hold all (to include feminine) a womb and birth would not be possible. God, however, is All That Is. Another feminine aspect of God we find in Proverbs 3:13-18 is wisdom,

Blessed are those who find wisdom, those who gain understanding, for she is more profitable than silver and yields better returns than gold. She is more precious than rubies; nothing you desire can compare with her. Long life is in her right hand; in her left hand are riches and honor. Her ways are pleasant ways, and all her paths are peace. She is a tree of life to those who take hold of her; those who hold her fast will be blessed.

If I am taught from a small child that God is a father and I have what I consider a loving father, this will probably set well in my psyche and be a positive experience for me. However, if my father was what I consider to be a bad one, harsh, distant, or even absent, then this belief will impact my life very differently than the former. And since, as stated earlier, we divide characteristics amongst males and females, i.e., feminine to females and masculine ones to males, other problems are likely to arise when a person's dominant characteristics don't match what society deems appropriate.

Sidebar: Nature's Dance of Masculine and Feminine Energies

Consider the animal kingdom: the lioness fiercely hunts and defends her pride, and the mother bear protects her cubs with bold strength, females expressing traditionally masculine qualities of action and protection.

Now look to the bird kingdom: many male birds such as the peacock and the birds of paradise, display vibrant colors and perform elaborate dances to attract mates. Expressions of beauty, allure, and emotional display, traditionally viewed as feminine traits.

In nature, masculine and feminine energies are not fixed by gender. They flow through all beings, depending on the situation, purpose, and expression. However, in our society this natural flow has been blocked by rigid unwritten rules or beliefs. Men are allowed to be angry or happy. Other emotions are deemed feminine and even wrong for them to feel. Sadness, fear, vulnerability, confusion, emotional pain, are often shut down in young boys by the adults around them. As they grow into men these emotions become uncomfortable for them to navigate and are repressed.

Women are freer to express a wider range of emotions without criticism. However, they face the stigma of being labeled "too" emotional if they do so often. When in a position

31

of authority, many women feel they have to compromise themselves to be respected or taken seriously.

Emotions should not be attributed to biological sex and should be regulated (or balanced) in everyone. Emotions are guides and are a direct line of communication from God within us. When we learn how to identify and express them beneficially, we can use them to work through challenges.

"Your emotions are your indicators of the vibrational alignment or misalignment with your Source energy. When you feel joy, love, or passion, you are in perfect alignment with who you really are. When you feel negative emotion, it is your indicator that you are focused on something that is out of alignment with your true self. Your emotions are your guidance system, always showing you the direction of your thoughts." —Abraham, as channeled by Esther Hicks

5 Communing with the Divine

"I will pour out my Spirit on all people. Your sons and daughters will prophesy, your old men will dream dreams, your young men will see visions. Even on my servants, both men and women, I will pour out my Spirit in those days."
—Joel 2:28-29

When I was a Christian, I remember wishing that there were still an open line of communication with "the other side" as there was with the prophets. I also wondered why angels were not still visiting earth as with Joseph and Mary and such. When I asked a minister, I was told, "This is not necessary since the fullness of God was revealed in His son Jesus." I remember thinking that it would still be nice to have.

I had heard of people who claimed to be channels, mediums, and psychics but I was taught that these were witchcraft and divination. These practices were presented to me through the eyes of the religion which deemed them Satanic. So, the committed Christian I was, I asked no more, looked no further than what I was told by the church and accepted it as my own belief. After all, I believed that these were God's laws.

However, in addition to my visions, I personally experienced times when I received audible messages, had telepathic type communication, dreams, and perceptions that I did not understand. Though these events were not scary, nor did they have the slightest feeling of evil attached to them, they weren't something I even thought about discussing. On one hand I didn't want people to think I was crazy, and from what I had been taught, I also didn't want to "give the devil a foothold."

Today, I understand the symptoms of psychosis, and I know this also does not fit my experiences.

With the information I was presented, I decided to obey the teachings of the church and ignore my own innate ability. I never learned to nurture the talents God had given me, and sadly, my spiritual gifts were weakened. I feel that I still have this ability to hear messages from what might be called *guides*, but because I was conditioned to believe that this kind of contact was demonic or mental illness at such an early age, currently my communication is shotty at best. However, through meditation I am working to restore my gifts and have had some success.

Perhaps you've also wondered why this kind of communication from "the other side" seemed to suddenly stop. If you were to ask ten different teachers from ten different religious traditions, you'd likely hear ten different explanations, each one confidently offered as the absolute truth. This led me to begin my own search, determined to explore the answers for myself and come to my own understanding.

Specifically, I wanted to know more about channeling and why it is considered a practice in opposition to God today, as it was clear to me in scripture that the prophets and priests utilized it often. As we have already established, God is *All That Is*, let us understand then that nothing is outside of God. It is only that the majority of humans, for several reasons over time, have been miseducated, and not knowing it, have in turn miseducated others. "The parents eat sour grapes, and the children's teeth are set on edge (Ezekial 18:2)."

For centuries, people have placed religious and political leaders between themselves and God. Elevating external authority above their own inner guidance. This dynamic has led most individuals away from the divine connection within themselves.

A clear example is found in the history of the Church during the Middle Ages, when access to scripture was restricted and only clergy were considered capable of interpreting God's word. People were taught to rely on someone else to mediate their relationship with the Divine. In modern times, we see a similar pattern, whether it's following the doctrine of a charismatic pastor without question or placing blind faith in political figures to define moral and spiritual truth. In both cases, the power to connect with God directly is outsourced, often silencing the still, small voice inside of each of us. True spiritual growth begins when we remember that inner guidance is not only valid, but sacred.

When you close your eyes to pray, who do you see in your mind's eye?

Though there were no cameras around when Source created life, if we are being honest, millions of people hold the image in their minds of a White, grey-haired male, in heaven or some distant realm of existence, passing judgment on each of us one at a time. Or perhaps you envision the man we call Jesus, as a flawless young White male with long hair, as depicted in thousands of pictures and movies. And when you understand the power of thought, this view was not presented to the masses by accident. If we are to start consuming solid food, we have got to let go of these images they were never true.

We are trained from small children to blindly trust and rely on leadership with God's name mixed in it. We easily accept what we are told because we are so young, and the information is taught to us by people we trust (parents, grandparents, ministers).

35

This programming is so subtle that even the most intelligent scholars among us don't realize they have been miseducated. Some will even argue to support misguided information without researching it for themselves. When some of us do ask questions, we get responses such as; *"Don't question God. Some things are beyond our understanding. God's ways are not our ways. The Lord works in mysterious ways."* and so on. Though each of these responses have truth, they are not true of everything we wish to know. Some of our questions do have valid answers that we are ready to comprehend.

Why would the people we love steer us wrong?

I'm reminded of a simple yet powerful parable: *A child was given a puzzle to complete. They worked at it for hours, struggling to make the pieces fit, growing more frustrated by the minute. Eventually, the child went to their parent in tears, saying, "I've tried everything, but I just can't do it, it doesn't work.' The parent looked at the puzzle and, with gentle compassion said, 'Oh sweetheart, no wonder, it's not your fault. I gave you the wrong pieces."*

That story has stayed with me because it so clearly mirrors what many of us go through. We are handed a set of beliefs, rules, and expectations, often from family, religion, or society, and told that if we follow them, life will make sense. But what happens when those pieces don't fit the deeper questions stirring within us? What happens when we try to build a picture of truth using fragments that were never meant for the puzzle our soul came here to solve?

Just like the child, I realized that some of the pieces I'd been given, while well-intended, didn't fit the picture of divine truth I was beginning to glimpse. And it wasn't until I stopped trying to force them into place that I began to find the pieces that did fit. The ones that came from within. The ones that connected me directly to God, not through a middleman, but through the quiet knowing of my own soul.

The teaching that the Bible (or any religious doctrine for that matter) is the *only* word of God, is another result of miseducation. And when one is active in a religion you are strongly discouraged from studying anything outside of what that religion approves of. So this was difficult for me to swallow at first, but the evidence became too overwhelming to deny. Of course, I had been warned about false teachers and prophets, that the devil is tricky, that in the last days scoffers would come, and so on (2 Peter 3 and Matthew 24).

When I held the belief that reading other perspectives is the "devil's work" then of course I obeyed. From what I had been taught about this Satan, he was for sure someone I didn't want to get caught up with. As a student of the Bible however, I also believed "For by him all things were created, in heaven and on earth, visible and invisible, whether thrones or dominions or rulers or authorities, all things were created through him and for him (Colossians 1:16)." If this is correct, how can there truly be another power in opposition to God (i.e., a Satan or devil)? It is likely there is another meaning lost in translation here. There are not two powers, God is the only power.

This understanding brought me a deep sense of comfort and freedom, permission to explore these concepts more openly, along with my personal relationship to them. After all, they exist, and nothing exists outside of God. This includes not only the beautiful and uplifting aspects of life, but also the parts we tend to reject, the uncomfortable, the shadowy, the things we might call unlovely or even evil. If all things come through God, then perhaps even these serve a purpose we don't yet fully understand. This perspective led me to

37

curiosity, compassion, and ultimately away from fear, allowing a more complete connection with our Source.

Sidebar: The Night Terror That Freed Me

In the initial stages of my research, I struggled deeply to reconcile the new information I was uncovering (new to me, though ancient in origin) with the teachings I had received in church. I had been so thoroughly conditioned to believe in the devil and his power that a part of me clung tightly to fear. I couldn't help but wonder if I were being deceived, just as I had been warned would happen.

Then one morning, after months of intense study, I experienced what I initially thought was a dream, only to later realize it was something else entirely. I believed I had woken up, but I was still lying on my back, paralyzed and overwhelmed by terror. My heart pounded wildly, and I struggled to breathe.

When I opened my eyes, I was met with a horrifying sight: a grotesque, wolf-like, demonic human figure was on top of me, staring into my eyes. He scowled, drooled, and grunted, his sharp teeth bared and dripping with blood and mucus. I was frozen, consumed by fear, but instinctively 3 times I repeated, "In the name of Jesus, I rebuke you." After the third time, the entity suddenly evaporated and I snapped out of the experience, this time truly awake.

As terrifying as that encounter was, nothing had really happened. The being hadn't harmed me at all; it had only breathed in my face. My inner guidance later revealed the truth: that monstrous figure was a projection born from my own fearful thoughts and deeply embedded false beliefs. It wasn't real. That's why it evaporated.

The power I invoked through utilizing the name of Jesus helped because of my beliefs around it at the time. However, as I developed my personal connection with the Creator, I was made aware that the power remains in me without having to invoke a mediator (I and my Father are One), which I believe is what the man we call Jesus was teaching us to understand. The experience was a turning point, showing me how controlling the mind can be, and how fear, left unchecked, can take on a life of its own.

SOPHIA C. RUSSELL

6 The Evolution of Sacred Texts

"Woe to you experts in the law, because you have taken away the key to knowledge. You yourselves have not entered, and you have hindered those who were entering." —Luke 11:52

As a Christian I was taught to believe that the collection of 66 books that make up the Holy Bible, written by at least 40 different human authors, over the course of approximately 4,000 years, are ultimately just one book inspired by one author—God.

The history and development of the Bible we have today is complex and as stated, it includes many contributions spanning over thousands of years. So without going into a complete history of how it was put together (as that would take writing another book) I offer a very brief and simplistic overview of the process below. To learn more, you can begin your study by looking up The Council of Nicaea, Pope Damasus, Emperor Constantine, and the canonization of the Bible to start.

Since the beginning of humanity, people have kept records about the creation of the universe, the beginning of Earth and man, messages about morality, right and wrong, their own cultural history, spiritual beliefs, and their gods. These are abundant and also include teachings from various leaders such as Buddha, Muhammad, Confucius, and the man we call Jesus, just to name a few. These texts are numerous and span the globe. Though they vary by culture and geographical location and the people gave God different names, many have eerily similar stories. One common among all of them is that beings came from the sky.

41

In the year 325 AD (that's three hundred and twenty-five years after the man we call Jesus left Earth) church leaders, about two to three hundred bishops, gathered under the direction of Emperor Constantine in what is now İznik, Turkey. This meeting is known as the Council of Nicaea, and their aim was to settle important questions about who the man we call Jesus was. At the time, most people saw him as another prophet, teacher, or messenger, and it was this council who officially declared him as divine, **THE** Christ.[5]

These church councils were made up of all male bishops of varying cultural backgrounds who held their own beliefs, ideas, and agendas. In the years that followed, several of these councils continued to convene, shaping core beliefs and determining how the religion would be structured, and to establish one doctrine to present to the people as the foundation of Christianity.

Participants, who were appointed by the church bishops, began sorting through thousands of ancient texts to decide which to include in this new doctrine. The books that were to be included had to go through a sanctioned approval process by these councils, *canonization*. This process took place over hundreds of years, and at each interval these men spent time discussing which texts would be included and perhaps more importantly, which texts *they believed* should be excluded.[6] [7]

This process also involved interpreting and translating, which once completed also had to be approved. Because these councils made these decisions for us, there are thousands upon thousands of writings we will never see and vast amounts of

---

[5] González. *The Story of Christianity, Volume 1.* (2010).

[6] Ehrman. *Lost Christianities: The Battles for Scripture and the Faiths We Never Knew.* (2003).

[7] Pagels. *The Gnostic Gospels.* (1979).

information that is not known by or taught in the churches, no matter which religion.

Many of these ancient texts are kept in storage in an acknowledged but restricted library at the Vatican, which is said to hold over 50 miles of shelving. Additionally, there were also thousands of ancient writings that had yet to be discovered at that time.

Bart D. Ehrman author and graduate of Princeton Theological Seminary discusses these limitations and others in his controversial book *Misquoting Jesus*, where he notes the complaints verbalized by translators, "We don't even have the first copies of the originals... these copies all differ from one another, in many thousands of places." [8]

Let me also note here, of those texts that were approved, upon translation it was common practice that if translators did not fully understand a passage, or had too much difficulty translating, they would just leave it out.

"The Life and Morals of Jesus of Nazareth," commonly referred to as the Jefferson Bible, is one of two religious works constructed by our third president and founding father, Thomas Jefferson. Jefferson (known as the primary author of the Declaration of Independence) compiled the manuscripts but never published them. The first, 'The Philosophy of Jesus of Nazareth" was completed in 1804, but no copies exist today. However, *The Life and Morals* was later published and is still available.

Here is a full quote from Jefferson's letter to John Adams on January 24, 1814, which later informed his manuscript,

---

[8] Ehrman. *Misquoting Jesus: The Story Behind Who Changed the Bible and Why.* (2005).

"The whole history of these books [the Gospels] is so defective and doubtful that it seems vain to attempt minute enquiry into it: and such tricks have been played with their text, and with the texts of other books relating to them, that we have a right, from that cause, to entertain much doubt what parts of them are genuine.

In the New Testament there is internal evidence that parts of it have proceeded from an extraordinary man; and that other parts are of the fabric of very inferior minds. It is as easy to separate those parts, as to pick out diamonds from dunghills."

Jefferson recognized that within the Bible are deeply profound truths yes, but also extensive portions of distortion and embellishment, either by human error or corruption, or perhaps some of both.[9]

Before moving on, let's take a little bit of a deeper dive into this timeline. Three hundred and twenty-five years AFTER the man we call Jesus left Earth, various writings about him, his relationship to God, scrolls and tablets which were written about God and creation, which spanned a timeframe of roughly four THOUSAND years, were gathered up and sorted through.

Imagine someone finding information about you three hundred years from now and ponder how accurate it might be. Or better yet, let's say 300 years from now someone is writing about Michael Jackson, after all that should be easier since he is so famous. However, since we have lived during the time of MJ we have an idea how even we, who are alive during his

---

[9] Jefferson. *The Life and Morals of Jesus of Nazareth.* (Compiled 1820).

lifetime, do not really know how much of what is written about him is accurate.

Though this example might be abstract, I say this for my reader (you) to ponder the doctrine by which you base your life. The Bible, as obviously useful as it is, has not gone untampered by men who had an agenda.

Our Source (God) however, is not bound by this doctrine, and you have a direct line of communication with God within your own heart and mind. "The coming of the kingdom of God is not something that can be observed, nor will people say, 'Here it is,' or 'There it is,' because the kingdom of God is in you (Luke 17:20-21)." "Do you not know that your body is a temple of the Holy Spirit, who is in you, whom you have received from God (1Corinthians 6:19)?"

When we accept the Bible (or any single religious doctrine) as the only word of God, it leads to two significant limitations:

1. It implies that we are forever bound by the choices of ancient gatekeepers who decided long ago what should and should not be included in sacred teachings.
2. It suggests that the Infinite Creator has only ever spoken through one source, in one moment of history, leaving no room for ongoing revelation, personal experience, or divine communication beyond that text.

Additionally, for those in the United States, the Bible and Christianity were brought over by Europeans, who imposed (forcibly) the religion and doctrine onto other cultures, completely disregarding that culture's established beliefs as valid.

In his log, Christopher Columbus made several observations about the Indigenous people he encountered during his voyages to the Americas. In particular, he believed that the native populations would be easily subdued and converted to Christianity, largely because he perceived them as naïve, peaceful, and lacking in military power or sophisticated defense strategies. Columbus described the indigenous people as "gentle and generous." [10]

He noted in his log that they did not have the kind of weaponry or military organization that would pose a serious threat to European conquerors. He even commented that with only a small number of men, he believed he could quickly dominate the native population, suggesting that they could easily be made subjects.

A famous entry from his log, dated October 12, 1492, when he first landed in the New World, reads: "They [the natives] would make fine servants... With fifty men we could subjugate them all and make them do whatever we want." [11]

While this view reflects Columbus's colonial ambitions and his underestimation of the complexities of native societies, it also foreshadowed the tragic consequences of European colonialism: the exploitation, subjugation, and eventual decimation of Indigenous populations through violence, enslavement, and disease. I do not even have to begin discussing the enslavement of Africans and all of the horrific actions inflicted over hundreds of years in this country and around the world. All while using the Bible and Christianity as support for "righteousness."

Deuteronomy 6:14, "Do not follow other gods, the gods of the peoples around you."

---

[10] Zinn. A People's History of the United States. (2005).
[11] de las Casas, *A Short Account of the Destruction of the Indies*. (1992).

This passage clearly states the existence of other deities that were worshipped by surrounding cultures. Not just idols, but "gods" with names and attributes. In today's society most of us have collectively left behind or do not even know our own connection with Source, because we were trained from birth of what religion or "god" to worship.

Stay with me.

Today, people often say, "Well, they weren't acting like true Christians." But in their own minds they believed they were. They truly thought they were serving God and that those who looked, lived, or worshipped differently weren't just mistaken, but deserving of judgment, enslavement, brutality, and even death.

One might say, "Well, I'm not the kind of Christian who would ever support violence against another human being" and that may be completely true. But it's still worth asking, what am I supporting? Because the foundation of many mainstream organized religions is separation from another group, not unity. And yet, God is Unity.

This separation may show up in many subtle ways. Statements like "We are the chosen ones'" or "Only *this* path leads to salvation." It shows up in subtle exclusions, such as judging someone for how they dress, who they love, or what they call God. It also shows up in traditions that promote fear of other faiths or discourage questioning. Over time, these beliefs form walls between people who are all, at their core, seeking the same Divine connection.

When we uphold systems that divide, no matter how passively, we may unknowingly block the very unity we claim to believe in. True spirituality, I've come to understand, does not separate. It welcomes; it includes. It sees God in all. "Through him all things were made; without him nothing was made that has been made (John 1:3)." And "… it was fitting that God, for whom and through whom everything exists…" Hebrews 2:10

Everything is God's Word.

Let's look at the various ways to define the word 'word.'

- a single distinct meaningful element of speech or writing used with others to form a sentence.
- a tool used to communicate or convey thoughts, ideas, and meaning.
- an order or command.

With our common sense we can deduce that at its origin God was not speaking any human language to create the universe and all it contains, so we can bypass the first definition and look at the other two. It makes more sense that God's tool to communicate (convey thoughts and meaning) is through creation, or the last one. God gave the order or command, and all of creation was produced.

This means God's word, includes the Bible, but God's word is not limited to it. God's word cannot be limited within the confines of a book cover. It is my guess that perhaps those individuals who hold that the Bible is the *only word* of God, are confusing our daily use of the word "word" found in the first definition above, with the other ways of defining it. This is another example of how the original meaning gets lost in translation.

Can you imagine if other fields of learning operated this way? Such as science, physics, or mathematics. We would consider the teacher or professor a fool if she/he used a book from the year 1700 saying it is all she needs, and that it is the

ONLY book necessary to learn all we need to know about any subject. However, we easily accept this belief about the Bible.

The Bible is one source of reading and learning about God, but it is not the only one. Just as it is impossible to place all of mathematics into one book, neither can we put all of God into one book. "Jesus did many other things as well. If every one of them were written down, I suppose that even the whole world would not have room for the books that would be written (John 21:25)."

Now, if it is impossible to gather all that the man we call Jesus did in one lifetime of 33 years and put it into a book, why do we think we can do so with the timelessness of God?

7 The Hidden Thread: The Science of The Invisible

"When you think of the mind-boggling expanse of our creation and the infantile state of our knowledge in relation to it, you begin to see the necessity for considering the strong probability that our present scientific approach to investigating these expanses is as primitive as the dugout canoe."
—*Don Elkins, 1984*

The true age of the universe remains unknown, while the Earth is estimated to be over 4 billion years old. In that vast span of time, how many intelligent human or human-like civilizations have risen and fallen? We may never know for sure, but archaeological evidence strongly suggests that there were many before us.

As I mentioned earlier, there are ancient texts and writings that predate the Bible by centuries, even millennia. Yet many Christians are conditioned to believe that the Bible is the only valid source of truth, and that any other account is automatically false, myth, invalid, or may even be labeled satanic. This kind of rigid thinking limits deeper exploration and keeps us from engaging with the broader tapestry of spiritual knowledge. True wisdom invites curiosity, not fear. It evolves beyond dogma and seeks to understand, not just to defend.

The Cuneiform tablets, also known as the Sumerian Tablets of Mesopotamia (which I will discuss more later) were famously unearthed in the late 1700's. To date the number of tablets found is roughly 1 million or more, and though mainstream scholars date them to about 3000 BC, experts in the field such as author and researcher Zecharia Sitchin, who spent over 40 years deciphering the texts, date them to more than 400,000 years old.

Though the age of these texts is disputed among scholars, it is agreed that the Sumerians are among the earliest known civilizations to exist. Some researchers have pointed out striking similarities between stories in the Bible and these much older texts, leading to the belief that parts of the Bible may have been "adapted" from the Cuneiform writings. [12] [13]

Accounts written down on these tablets, such as the creation story, the flood, and others, hold an eerie likeness to scripture, with a lot more detail and less mysticism. In my view, many of the Biblical stories were not just "adapted" but *plagiarized* from these tablets. However, I am told that saying parts of the Bible are plagiarized would be incorrect. Not because this wasn't done, but because being so long ago there were no laws in place which kept someone from taking another's writing and claiming it as their own. Additionally, many Biblical books have no known author and scholars offer educated guesses on who the writer may have been.

God, our Source, however, is not stagnant sitting in the pages of a book. God is ever expanding, growing, and experiencing Itself by manifesting as you and me, and all of creation. Source continues to communicate with us through Its creation, of which you are a part, in innumerable ways. The Bible is one way, there are other texts, experience is another, through other people is yet another, and there are many more. However, the absolute best way to commune with God, is to go within. But we have been programmed that we are "sinners" and not to trust ourselves, to look outward for God.

In John 14, when the man we call Jesus said, "I Am the way the truth and the life" he was teaching us to repeat this

---

[12] Sitchin. *The 12th Planet*. (1976).
[13] Kramer. *The Sumerians: Their History, Culture, and Character*. (1963).

phrase, to imitate his way, to literally *DO* what he did, not to worship him. The *I Am* is God residing in each of us, when we say, I Am, whatever we say after is proclaimed, and is the beginning of manifesting. The sad part is, without having this knowledge we often proclaim things we do not want. "I am sick, I am ugly, I am broke," etc. Not realizing that as we think and believe, we are giving commands to the Universe and are taking an active part in creating these experiences for ourselves.

The Invisible and Visible

Before I began studying universal laws, I often wondered why "bad" things seemed to happen to "good" people, while those who appeared to do wrong often seemed unbothered or even blessed. It didn't make sense, until I started to understand the deeper truth about energy. That's where the answers began to unfold.

If we could observe our bodies under an extremely powerful microscope, beyond cells and down to the atomic and subatomic level, we would see that what appears to be solid matter is actually made up of rapidly vibrating particles. These particles, such as atoms and the subatomic components within them (protons, neutrons, and electrons), are in constant motion. In fact, 99.9999% of what we perceive as "solid" is actually empty space, with energy fields and vibrational frequencies holding the structure together.

From a scientific standpoint, this aligns with principles in quantum physics, which reveal that matter is not truly solid in the way our senses perceive it. Instead, it is energy condensed into a specific vibrational form. Every object and living being emits a frequency (*a measurable result of the rate at which its particles vibrate*). These frequencies interact with the environment and even with the frequencies of other people, objects, and natural forces.

Our eyes interpret this energy as physical because of how our sensory systems are tuned to interact with the material world. But in truth, we are dynamic, energetic beings in constant motion, vibrations made visible through the lens of consciousness and perception. This is the same principle that explains how everything in the universe, from rocks to stars to human bodies, is composed of vibrating energy fields, each radiating a unique frequency in the grand symphony of existence.

As Gary Zukav discusses in *The Dancing Wu Li Masters*, and Fritjof Capra elaborate in *The Tao of Physics*, matter is not static but is, in fact, a dynamic web of energy, interconnected and in perpetual motion, reminding us that what we call "solid" is just energy, vibrating at a frequency our senses can perceive. [14] [15]

The Laws of Vibration & Attraction: Energetic Alignment and the Power of Frequency

When we begin to truly understand ourselves as energetic beings, it becomes clear that our thoughts and emotions emit vibrational frequencies that influence our external reality, and we can feel it. When you're consumed by intense anger or emotional agony, you emit a powerful and concentrated energetic frequency. In those heightened states, a tremendous amount of energy surges out from you in a short span of time. Once the emotional wave passes and you begin to calm down, you often feel drained or depleted. It's common to say, "I don't

---

[14] Capra. *The Tao of Physics: An Exploration of the Parallels Between Modern Physics and Eastern Mysticism.* (1991).
[15] Zukav. The Dancing Wu Li Masters. (2001).

have any energy" because in truth, your energetic body has been temporarily exhausted by the outflow.

By consciously aligning our internal frequency with the energy of the experiences we desire instead, we direct that energetic flow into a more enlightened state, becoming powerful co-creators of our lives. For example, if I choose to embody the mindset and emotions of someone who is already wealthy, feeling abundant, secure, and grateful, even in the absence of physical evidence, I begin to resonate with the frequency of wealth. Over time, this alignment attracts circumstances, ideas, and opportunities that mirror that frequency, allowing wealth to express itself through me.

Conversely, if I dwell in the belief that I am lacking or poor, and allow feelings of scarcity, fear, or unworthiness to dominate, I emit a frequency that attracts more of the same. The outer world simply reflects the inner signal I am transmitting.

Also, be mindful of the tendency to "feel sorry" for others. While it may seem empathetic to feel bad for someone who is suffering, this reaction does not truly serve them. When you align emotionally with their pain, you unintentionally amplify it by matching and reinforcing the frequency of their struggle. This can make it even harder for them to rise above it. Instead, offer your presence, your listening ear, and your genuine support. Be sensitive, yes, but hold a higher vision for them. In your heart and mind, see them whole, strong, and in the process of healing. Feel that reality as if it's already happening. This subtle energetic support helps create a pathway for their recovery and transformation.

It's important to understand that in our current dimensional experience, bound by time and space, these energetic shifts are not always instantaneous. It takes time for the momentum of a new frequency to build and for reality to reorganize itself around that new energetic pattern. Patience, consistency, and belief are key to sustaining that vibrational shift until it is reflected in physical form.

This is the deeper meaning behind Matthew 13:12: "For whoever has, to him more will be given, and he will have abundance; but whoever does not have, even what he has will be taken away."

In this verse, the man we call Jesus is describing what we now understand as the Law of Attraction and the Law of Vibration. The idea that what we internally align with is what we draw into our external reality. [16]

When I talk about energy, frequency, and vibration, some people tell me it sounds more scientific than spiritual. But it is all the same, because God, our Source, is the very fabric of energy that makes up everything, thus everything is spiritual. These aren't separate ideas; they're just different concepts pointing to the same truth.

The problem is, we've been conditioned to see our spiritual world only through the lens of religion, so we often miss the deeper connections. We think we have a "regular" life and a "spiritual" life. We compartmentalize science, technology, evolution, spirituality, and creationism, not realizing they are all expressions of the same Divine Intelligence.

Indigenous cultures and native peoples all over the world and throughout time understand this unity far better than we do in contemporary society. They don't separate science from spirit or nature from the Divine. To them, the movement of the stars, the cycles of the moon, the rhythms of the body, the

---

[16] Hicks and Hicks. *The Law of Attraction: The Basics of the Teachings of Abraham.* (2006).

patterns of nature, and the flow of energy are all sacred, they are all part of the same living intelligence that we call God, Source, the Universe, or All That Is.

Whether through meditation, ceremony, or studying the natural world, we should seek alignment with that greater rhythm, not dominion over it. Knowledge is intuitive, experiential, and deeply integrated. But when we are trained to be "civilized" much of this wisdom is dismissed, buried, or labeled as primitive, myth, or heretical by systems that prioritize control over connection. But the truth doesn't disappear, it just waits for us to remember.

8 Who Actually *Owns* the Word?

"Unlike so many, we do not peddle the word of God for profit. On the contrary, in Christ we speak before God with sincerity, as those sent from God."
—*2 Corinthians 2:17*

We often hear that the Bible is the "inspired Word of God." A sacred text to be revered, studied, and obeyed. But few of us ever stop to ask a very practical question: Who actually *owns* the rights to it? Not metaphorically, but legally, financially, and corporately.

With over 5 billion copies sold and millions more distributed every year, the Bible isn't just a holy manuscript, it's a global industry. And like any industry, it has gatekeepers, publishers, and power players, many of whom have little spiritual interest in the text itself.

After all, this is THE best-selling book of ALL TIME, with approximately 54,945 sold every day around the world. That's about 2,289 sold per hour, 38 per minute, and 6.4 Bibles sold every 10 seconds. The average Bible cost about $40, when I do the math, that's over $2 million a day, over $800 million a year. Have you ever thought about who is profiting?

Let's briefly discuss two which are among the highest selling versions, the King James (KJV) and the New International (NIV).

According to standard copyright law, the original 1611 King James Version (KJV) of the Bible is in the public domain in most countries, including the United States, because it is centuries old. However, in the United Kingdom, the rights to print and reproduce the KJV are held under a royal prerogative

59

known as the Crown Copyright. This special right has been maintained since the time of King James I and is still administered today by the Queen's (now King's) printer and it is renewed upon the accession of each new monarch. Therefore, within the UK, reproducing the KJV requires paying for a license from the Crown.

The New International Version (NIV), the second bestselling Bible in the world, is published by Zondervan in the United States. Zondervan is a prominent Christian publishing company that, along with Thomas Nelson, is owned by HarperCollins Christian Publishing. HarperCollins itself is a subsidiary of News Corp, the global media conglomerate founded by Rupert Murdoch. Through this corporate structure, Murdoch's media empire oversees one of the world's largest producers of Bibles and bestselling Christian books.

Now the average person may say, "Well good for the royal family and Murdoch. They are doing something godly by making sure that '*God's Word*' or the Bible is published and distributed."

But let's be real, these are savvy businesspeople, they couldn't care any less about the masses knowing God. The Bible is a billion-dollar industry which has created generational wealth for their families dating back centuries. As long as the masses (you and I) believe that the Holy Bible is the only word of God they will continue profiting handsomely for generations to come.

It is in their best interest to keep us believing that God is outside while remaining clueless to God residing inside of us. Their profit margin would quickly dwindle if the majority knew that we only need to go within ourselves. And if that doesn't grab you, these same corporations (or publishers underneath their umbrella) are also among the largest selling producers of the Satanic Bible as well.

If the Bible is inspired by God, why so many versions and new editions?

Publishers often explain that these updates are necessary to reflect changes in language and improve readability. While this may be true to an extent, there is also a financial incentive. Each time a new individual or organization produces a translation, they secure the copyright to that version. Given that the Bible remains the best-selling book of all time, a well-marketed translation can generate substantial income into their organization for generations to come.

The Word of God Is Everywhere

While the Bible is certainly revered, again, it is not the only way God speaks to us. Church leaders use the Bible as the foundation for their teachings, yes, but as they teach, they also present their own interpretations of scripture and share personal experiences as expressions of God's word. Additionally, divine communication often comes in subtle unexpected ways, tucked into ordinary moments.

A loved one's presence felt in a time of need. A whisper in the morning that wakes you just in time. An urge to turn left instead of right, only to later realize you avoided harm. A stir of inspiration in your soul while sitting alone on a park bench, or the infectious laughter of a child that suddenly lifts your heavy heart. Artists often describe their work as something that flows through them, as though the song, music, or painting came from somewhere beyond what they can explain.

Since my father's passing in 2008, I've felt his presence more than once. And there have been times when my mother's photo randomly appeared on my phone screen, like a soft nudge from the other side reminding me that her love never dies. Maybe you too have had similar experiences. These moments defy logic but speak deeply to the unseen world.

In my view, these are all ways God communicates. Not always through scripture or sermons, but through life itself. Through love, instinct, nature, and intuition −the quiet knowing within. The language of God is not confined to one book or one voice. It's everywhere, speaking always, for those who are open to listening. "Whoever has ears, let him hear." Matthew 11:15, Matthew 13:9, Mark 4:9, 23, and Revelation 2:7, 11, 17, 29; 3:6, 13, 22; 13:9

We often brush off these moments of divine synchronicity as mere coincidences or strokes of luck. Others may quickly cast doubt, suggesting that we can't truly know the source, implying that it could be some other spirit, and not actually God at all. But this kind of thinking reflects more fear than faith.

However, I do understand why people sometimes react this way and I'll explore that shortly, but for now I'll simply remind you: God is All That Is. Everything that is, is created through Source, and nothing has been created without Source. Rather we in our human understanding view it as positive or negative, it is still from God, and our comprehension of this is what makes the experience beneficial or not.

The Bible is a done deal; it gets edited but never added to. In truth, aside from the many writings that did not make it in, several books and passages have been removed from it since its initial edition. And depending upon a person's particular type of Christianity (i.e., Catholic, Baptist, Jehovah's Witness, Methodist, Morman, Seventh Day Adventist, Non-

Denominational, etc.) their culture or where they live in the world, their version of the Holy Bible varies in its text. Additionally, anything written down ages ago and found today, as we discussed already, is open to interpretation by the professional who then conveys their understanding to you. I am not saying this is wrong, as I am doing the same thing here as I write this book.

What I am saying is that God has not left us solely dependent upon the reading of ancient texts or the Bible; to be the only way we learn about Creation and how to navigate our lives. Someone else's understanding should not replace my own, it should help me go within, keeping my own line open with the Source. God is in each one of us, and we do not need anything else but to connect with our own inner guidance. Again, this is the best way to commune with God.

"I will put my laws in their minds and write them on their hearts. I will be their God, and they will be my people. No longer will they teach their neighbor, or say to one another, 'Know the Lord,' because they will all know me, from the least of them to the greatest (Hebrews 8:10)."

Now I ask you, my brothers and sisters, *how* will you ever uncover what God has put in *your* mind and written on *your* heart, if you are only reading, studying, and repeating what someone else *told* you to believe, *told* you is right, *told* you is true?

9 Faith, Freedom, and the Veil

"My brothers and sisters, some from Chloe's household have informed me that there are quarrels among you. What I mean is this: One of you says, 'I follow Paul'; another, 'I follow Apollos'; another, 'I follow Cephas;' still another, 'I follow Christ.' Is Christ divided? Was Paul crucified for you? Were you baptized in the name of Paul?" —1Corinthians 1:11-13

The church community I was a member of was a very loving and supportive one. I fell in love with the cultural diversity and the commitment each member was called to, to genuinely follow Jesus, know your Bible, to "seek and save the lost," and to continuously work to better yourself.

The structure that was in place was based on the New Testament where we did not own buildings, and like the worshippers in the book of Acts we gathered in homes, rented facilities, and parks. It was a fairly large church as a whole and the members were geographically organized.

A hierarchy of leadership was placed over each area to help guide the members. Within those groups we were all assigned what was called a "discipleship partner." This was someone each of us learned to trust, respect, and confide in. As it was understood, we would all stumble at times or need guidance. Having a partner to talk with or confess to would help to get you back on your feet. Sounds great right? Well, being a committed member for about 20 years, I can say it was nice, and I personally grew to understand myself, God, and others while there. Today, I see the benefit of my life as a Christian and would never take it back.

However, among many of the faults with this lifestyle was the requisite to *always* seek advice. To me, this was one of a few areas where things got murky. If one was considering moving, choosing a school, looking for a job, traveling, getting married, dating, anything! You were **strongly** encouraged to "seek advice" from within the church first.

If a member carried out any of these, and it was found that advice was not sought, it was heavily frowned upon. That member was often viewed as a problem. While I get the benefit of talking big decisions over with someone, the way this "seeking advice" was carried out was more like control, than advice giving.

At times members might consult with a close relative or other knowledgeable individuals, but if these people were not Christians, it was implied that their advice may not be the best. If someone needed therapy, they should seek out a Christian therapist, which is fine. But as a therapist myself, I am educated in and ethically bound to the practice of helping people in following guidance that is within their own belief system, not mine. If Christianity or any practice is important to a client, I offer healing techniques that honor that and would never seek to impose something different.

However, I have had clients who came to me *after* seeing a Christian therapist, who literally told them their difficulty was primarily due to the fact that they were living in "sin." While offering no practical guidance on how to change, this accusation was not only false but added to their mental distress. There is an enumerable amount of intelligent, loving people who offer sound advice, healing, and guidance from their wisdom, education, and knowledge without being Christian.

I am not saying that every person who calls themselves a Christian behaves this way or that it is wrong to claim this faith. I am simply hoping to wake you up to the frequency you are emitting by your underlying thoughts and beliefs. When I served as a Christian, I did so because I believed that it was the only way to serve God, and it is likely this is the reason most do. Through deeper study and awakening, I was enlightened, and I hope to enlighten others.

During his time on Earth, the man we call Jesus never referred to himself or his followers as "Christians." That label did not emerge until years after his departure. According to Acts 11:26, the disciples were first called Christians in the city of Antioch, a name most scholars believe was given by outsiders and may have originally been meant as an insult.

Again, the man we call Jesus did not give a formal *title* to those who followed his teachings, nor did he establish a religion or religious system. Instead, he invited people into deeper awareness, personal transformation, and unity with God and one another. He did not promote gathering on specific days or organizing religious meetings in the structured way we are all familiar with today.

In fact, this teacher often challenged the legalism of his time, especially around the Sabbath. On multiple occasions, this teacher purposely healed on the Sabbath, not to rebel, but to show that compassion, presence, and divine love transcend religious rules (see Mark 3:1–6 and Luke 13:10–17). His way was not about creating separation through labels or ritual but about restoring our direct connection with God.

When spiritual teachings urge us to be *in the world but not of it*, they're pointing to our inner life, that is our thoughts, beliefs, emotions, and behaviors. These should reflect higher truth rather than mirror the habits and mindset of the masses.

This matters because, again, our inner state emits a frequency that magnetizes experiences, drawing us into either harmony or disharmony.

Consider this: you lose your job. The natural reaction might be fear or anxiety, especially as time passes without any promising leads. Though outwardly you say things like, *"I know God is good."* Or *"Jesus will fix it"* etc.

How do you respond inwardly? Is there a sense of panic or heightened anxiety? When this happens do you truly lean into faith, trusting that God will open a path forward? You will know by the experience you are having, either continued struggle or the uplifting feeling that opportunity is on the horizon. Again these are felt, not said.

Or imagine a time period when everyone around you is consumed by the latest celebrity scandal. The media swirls with judgment, speculation, and opinion. Do you join in, adding your voice to the noise? If so, your attention aligns your vibration with the energy of gossip, criticism, and distraction. In doing so, you may unknowingly invite similar chaos into your own life. Your focus always sets the tone for what comes next.

In challenging situations, we can either react as most people do or choose to respond in ways that reflect our relationship with God. We are here in this world to learn how to make healthier, more constructive choices, responses that align us with our higher selves and support our spiritual growth, even if they differ from the people around us.

Looking back, I recall how many members of my church walked away from promising careers, some as athletes, entertainers, even doctors, to enter the ministry. During baptism preparation, it was common to be asked questions like, "If God called you to give up your singing career to serve Him, could you?" The underlying message was clear: *serving God* meant prioritizing church life and responsibilities above all else. This included daily Bible study, evangelizing, attending every church event, contributing financially, and focusing on "saving souls." Personal responsibilities (such as family, work, or self-care) were often considered secondary, and at times, even distractions from spiritual duty.

If the individual was hesitant or was not willing, it was concluded that they did not put God first, or that their career was more important to them than God. Typically, baptism was held off until they had a "change of heart." As a member of this church, I took on that belief as well, and instead of pursuing any other career, going into the ministry became my primary goal. I believed it was the best way to serve God.

As I began waking up however, I realized that God is the one who leads a person from the inside. If one feels called to be an athlete, entertain, heal others, or whichever career aligns with their own passion, it is between that person and God. "But in fact, God has placed the parts in the body, every one of them, just as he wanted them to be (1 Corinthians 12:18)."

By identifying and using our innate talents, we are each expressing the Creator in a way that only we can and should not have to change due to someone else's belief in what we *should* be doing. In The Parable of the Talents (Matthew 25) we are encouraged to boldly use the gifts God has entrusted to us, to cultivate and nurture them, and to return to the Source with increase, a divine return on Its investment.

Everything and everyone have come out of God just the way God created them to. But when we are part of a particular belief structure or organized religion, we are taught that *this* way is the *only and right* way and then directed to impose *our* way onto others. Holding firm in the belief that because what the other believes or does is different, they are not connected to God, and we are. We are "saved," and they are "lost." We are "righteous" and they are in "sin." This is the basis for many wars.

Eventually, I stopped attending that church. It wasn't a conscious decision at first, my life circumstances had shifted, and I relocated to another state, and lived in a very small town where there was not an official sister church of the branch I had belonged to. I visited a few churches in my new town, but over time I grew weary of the entire experience and decided to step away from the commitment. In hindsight, I now see that this move was divinely orchestrated, setting me on a new path.

Years later, I heard that the leadership of that once-thriving church—established back in the 1970s—had fallen into disagreement. The congregation eventually split into two or three separate churches, leaving members to choose which direction or leader to follow. I don't know all the details, but I imagine it was a challenging and painful experience for everyone involved.

The Veil of Forgetting

I inform you today my brothers and sisters, though it may feel like it at times, you are never at risk of being lost, you are always one with God. Remember these wise words in Psalm 23 "Though I walk through the valley of the shadow of death, I will fear no evil; For You are with me."

What you really are is asleep, and I hope to assist in waking you up. In truth before coming into your current life, you agreed to forget who you really are. You (we all) agreed to the "slumber" or the "spiritual amnesia" we are currently experiencing. Forgetting who we are before coming into this human experience is a crucial part of our journey and useful for our personal growth.

A key component in earning many academic degrees and certifications is how to conduct thorough and effective research. During my educational training, I explored various methods, and one that particularly stood out to me was the use of *blind studies.* In this context, the term *"blind"* refers to intentionally withholding information about treatment assignments from those involved in the study.

The method of *blinding* is used to reduce bias and ensure more accurate, objective results. It's based on the understanding that people often change their behavior when they know they are being watched or possess certain information. By keeping participants unaware that they are being studied or observed, their actions tend to be more natural, producing results that are more reliable and true to life.

A well-known example of this in practice is the television show Undercover Boss, which mirrors a single-blind study: employees behave as they normally would, unaware that the "new hire" is actually their CEO.

In much the same way, we enter this life under a "veil of forgetting." We don't remember our origins as souls, and that spiritual amnesia serves a purpose. It allows us to respond to life's challenges in a raw and authentic way, unshaped by the knowledge of who we've been before. In doing so, our true character emerges, not the one crafted by memory or expectation, but the one rooted in our present awareness. This setup provides the perfect environment for growth, transformation, and the unfolding of deeper wisdom.

As spiritual teachers, when we tell others what they "must" do or how they "must" behave, we risk disrupting their free will and personal growth, often unintentionally steering them off their unique path. Even when our intentions are good, our advice is usually filtered through our own beliefs, experiences, and perspectives. While someone else's situation may appear similar to ours, we cannot truly know what their soul came here to learn.

A more supportive approach is to ask thoughtful questions that help others access their own inner wisdom. This can be done by learning a method referred to as *Socratic Questioning*. Based on the approach of Socrates, these types of questions encourage individuals to explore their own thoughts, beliefs, motivations, and desires, helping them arrive at conclusions that align with their personal journey. Even if the choices they make lead to outcomes we might view as mistakes, the process of self-examination still offers valuable lessons and growth.

10 Clearing the Smoke of Fear

"For God has not given us a spirit of fear, but of power and of love and of a sound mind." —2 Timothy 1:7

Throughout history information about God and creation has always been communicated through various sources. Today, it is typically rediscovered through disciplines such as archeology and anthropology. It may be written down (such as hieroglyphs, ancient tablets, and scrolls), passed down from teacher to student (esoteric, such as the Kabbalah), and even communicated from "out there" to an individual. This is what religion calls prophesying, theologians call direct revelation, and what is also sometimes termed channeling.

In addition to the spiritual guidance we gain from the various sources mentioned already, there are also teachers from other realms of reality who have been communicating with us since the origin of humanity here on Earth. Because of the vast amounts of miseducation passed down from generation to generation, it is helpful to have access to these teachers and guides, as they are more than willing to help us.

They have never stopped speaking; it is just that we have been told they have, or that it is of the devil. And if you recall from scripture, it was the worshipers and the religious people of that time, those who claimed to be the most godly, who told the man we call Jesus that he was of the devil. Yet we sit comfortably in our religious beliefs behaving the same way without recognizing it.

As a holistic and alternative therapist, I sometimes give classes in order to assist others in understanding these concepts. As I journeyed from Christianity to a more unlimited view of the Creator, I was initially very afraid. Today, I found that there are many others who live with that same fear when seeking truth, especially when what we find does not align with what we have been programmed to believe. This realization can be even more difficult if you are leading a large congregation of Christians.

When we feel fear, we seem to immediately associate it with something harmful or evil, when in many cases it is simply miseducation. For example, in one class I was teaching about clearing a space with sage. Two women in the back row were obviously uncomfortable, their faces changed, they whispered something between them, and scooted the sage away as if it were poisonous.

Now if we remove any belief system, sage (which naturally grows out of the Earth) has long been revered for its healing and spiritual properties. Inhalation of its essential oils, especially through steam or aromatherapy, has been associated with stress reduction, mood improvement, and respiratory support, including relief from conditions like asthma and bronchitis. This is due to its anti-inflammatory and antimicrobial compounds.[17] [18]

When consumed properly (like in tea or food) sage is not only a very tasty seasoning, but has been shown to support cognitive health, digestion, and oral hygiene, while also acting as a natural anti-inflammatory. In holistic traditions, particularly among Indigenous and Earth-based cultures, burning sage (especially white sage) is used in ceremonies to purify and clear negative energy from a space.

---

[17] Kennedy, et al. *"Effects of Sage on Mood, Anxiety, and Performance in Human Volunteers."* (2006).

[18] Nautiyal et al. *"Medicinal Smoke Reduces Airborne Bacteria."* (2007).

These two women, I found out later, had not understood what class they signed up for, and they left shortly after the sage lesson. Because I had been a devout Christian for so many years myself, I did not judge their reaction. Afterall, I had held the same conviction at one time. I had been taught that burning sage was associated with the "dark arts" such as voodoo, spell casting, devil worship, etc. And I do not deny that it still is. However, someone else's use of sage does not negate the fact that I can use it in the "light arts" for cleansing purposes, setting my own loving intentions.

People also use money for dark or evil purposes, but I never hear a person say they will not use money because of this. What they might say is they would not use their money for evil but for good, and this is the same idea for anything God has created. Learn about its benefits before you shun it as evil. After all, scripture teaches us that the leaves are for the healing of the nations (Revelations 22:2).

The same idea is true regarding channeling. We read about the prophets channeling throughout the Bible, but in religion we do not use that word, we use the word prophesying. Miseducation around words and their differences in use can also send us running out of the classroom, however this is another way we close ourselves off from gaining useful knowledge.

Several days later, as I pondered how I could deliver this information in a class without people fleeing from the room, my higher guidance said, "Nothing needs to change about your class dear one. When you burned the sage, your intention cleared negative energy from your space. Thus, these women could not remain."

11 Healing in the Age of Skepticism

"The spirit is the life, the mind is the builder, the physical is the result." —Cayce Reading 262-3

Edgar Cayce (1877-1945) is arguably one of the most recognized modern day channelers. Known during his time as the "sleeping prophet" Cayce would be given the address (or location) of an ill person, lie down on his couch, close his eyes, and go into a sleeping state or trance. After a few moments, and while still in the trance, he verbally diagnosed the individual and gave remedies to cure the ailment.

His life's work has made a significant impact, not only in the metaphysical and alternative holistic communities, but also in mainstream medical science. However, his methods remain a mystery, scientific researchers tend to shun these types of phenomena sometimes labeling it as "pseudo psychology." Those few who step up to do more research often face adversity and are underfunded.

Many of the people whom Cayce helped had previously gone to numerous medical doctors with no answers or results before they turned to him as a last resort. After having what became known as a "reading" with him, in which their physical presence was not necessary, the individual not only received accurate insight into their illness but reported that after following his instructions the ailment was cured. Thousands of these cases were documented by physicians before and after seeing Cayce and also followed for several months (sometimes years) after being cured, to support the patients' claims.

Cayce had grown up in a devoted Christian family, and since a very young age he had not been the brightest student and struggled to retain the lessons taught in school. He had taken a keen interest in the Bible however, and while still in primary school, he had the revelation that he should have read the Bible for every year he was alive and did so. He continued this practice throughout his life and was known for proclaiming that he loved reading it so much. He said that his prayer ever since he was a young boy was to "help others like Jesus did."

When asked how he obtained this ability, Cayce would be happy to explain various mystical events he experienced throughout his childhood, especially a time when he was about 13 years old. He said a female apparition appeared before him surrounded by an all-encompassing bright light. She told him his prayer had been granted, that he should remain faithful and help others. He would admit, however, that he did not fully grasp what she meant at the time.

Soon after that event, Cayce's parents got a report from his school that he failed another spelling test. That evening his father stayed up late with the intention of helping his son memorize the words and pass the test. As the night grew later, his father became so exasperated with Cayce's inability to spell any of the words, that he struck the young boy knocking him out of his chair. Cayce, exhausted as well, reported that at that moment he heard the voice of the woman telling him to go to sleep with the book under his head, and she would assist him.

By then it was after 9 pm and Cayce asked his father for permission to take a short break. He explained that he was confident he would get it if he could rest for a few minutes. His father reported that after about 5 minutes he woke Cayce and recited one of the words for him to spell.

One by one, Cayce began spelling each word correctly, leaving his father astonished. Curious, his father pressed him for an explanation, and Cayce told him of the woman's instructions. To test his claim, his father flipped through the textbook, selecting random words for Cayce to spell, all of which he did accurately, even those the class hadn't yet covered.

Throughout the rest of his schooling Cayce continued this practice. By sleeping on his books, he absorbed the material and knew all the answers in class without studying.

As a young man he had his heart set on becoming a preacher or missionary, which according to his Christian influence were the best way of helping others. Though he experienced what would be called other "psychic events" throughout his young life, he gave his first reading for himself at about age 15. After being struck by a baseball and in pain, with his parents by his side he went into the trance and told them what should be done. His parents followed the direction of making a poultice to place on the affected area, and upon doing so for the time recommended in the reading, Cayce was healed. Still not realizing this as a gift, he used it sporadically.

It was not until he was about 24 years old that he met Dr. Al Layne, a local self-schooled osteopath and hypnotist. Dr. Layne had studied all the material necessary to become a doctor, but had not gone to a formal school, so though knowledgeable he was unlicensed.

At the time, Cayce was experiencing a severe case of laryngitis that left him unable to speak above a whisper for over a year. Layne offered to help Cayce using hypnosis, which eventually led to the discovery of Cayce's ability to give detailed medical readings while in a trance state.

Deeply fascinated by his diagnostic abilities while in this state, Layne ended up becoming one of Cayce's first collaborators. He was so impressed by the information Cayce gave that he began reporting to colleagues that Cayce spoke like an expert in medicine. He fluidly used medical terminology and expressed knowledge of biology and anatomy one only gets from several years of formal education.

Cayce, however, had only completed up to the ninth grade in a small schoolhouse in the country. Though he desired to go to college it was not affordable for his family, so he was unable to continue his education, and he had not studied any medical literature. Despite this limitation, while in trance he provided readings with sophisticated medical knowledge that went far beyond many who had obtained proper schooling, and Dr. Layne knew he was witnessing something miraculous.

It was Layne who initially encouraged Cayce to build a formal practice around using his gift, and the two began working together to treat various ailments for Layne's patients. This partnership marked the beginning of Cayce's medical readings and within a short time, the word of their small practice there in Hopkinsville, Kentucky spread.

As more and more doctors in the surrounding areas began losing patients, Layne & Cayce's practice only grew and it was not long before there was a buzz within the local medical community. For a fraction of the cost of seeing a doctor people were claiming to be cured, not medicated, by the use of all natural treatments. There was only a small fraction of cases (typically those who were far gone) where the minimal use of a pharmaceutical was suggested alongside the natural remedies.

Dr. Layne would sit with Cayce while in trance, ask the necessary questions, take notes, give them to patients, and then assist the patients in carrying them out. Sometimes the patients were present and sometimes they were not, either way Cayce was able to diagnose them and prescribe remedies that worked to completely restore health.

His remedies involved various kinds of herbal treatments, dietary suggestions, osteopathy, physical therapy, massage, exercise, rest, etc. Though today these kinds of recommendations are the norm, this was not the case in the early 1900's. Cayce has since been called the father of Holistic Medicine and many of his treatments have been studied and added into mainstream healing practices. After aiding many in his surrounding area, people from all over the country began either writing or coming to see him for a reading.

At one point a man, Arthur Lammers who was a mystic enthusiast, took interest in what he had heard about Cayce and approached him about discussing more than just illness while in this sleeping state. Out of his own love for God and curiosity about creation Cayce agreed, and through a series of readings Lammers questioned the sleeping man about the "secrets of the ages."

He queried about such subjects as creation, life after death, why we are here, reincarnation, and historical anomalies such as the building of the pyramids and the so-called lost cities like Atlantis. To everyone's astonishment, Cayce would share ageless wisdom and knowledge and a thorough understanding of all these topics.

A high percentage of these readings were transcribed and upon reviewing them Cayce himself would cringe. While he was in his waking state, he did not remember what was being said through him, and because of his Christian beliefs he often had difficulty with the information that was coming through. As any devout Christian would, he questioned the source hoping he was not carrying out the work of a devil.

Cayce was vigilant however, and because his work was helping so many people heal and live longer healthier lives, he knew it was from God. He regularly studied the scriptures alongside the information recorded in his readings, and along with Lammers, saw how the knowledge coming through, superseded and yet also threaded through all religious belief systems.

While in this trance state and under the questioning of Lammers, he was asked where this knowledge was coming from. Cayce explained that he was accessing what is called the *Akashic Record*, and described this as a universal, vibrational record of every soul's journey (past, present, and future). Some researchers note that this is likely what is referred to as "The Book of Life" in scripture.[19] [20]

This record is said to contain the history of every thought, action, and intent ever experienced by every soul. Cayce explained that these records are not written in physical form but exist in the etheric realm and can be accessed by anyone. However, a person must be attuned to higher levels of consciousness to tap into it. He emphasized that the Akashic Records are used by the soul between incarnations to review its growth and plan future lessons for spiritual evolution.

Cayce also explained the use and guidance of practices such as astrology and cosmology in human experience. He discussed intelligent life throughout the universe and how we transition in and out of various life experiences for growth and evolution with no death. He gave detailed descriptions that were documented about coming world events like The Great

---

[19] Edgar Cayce Readings. (ARE, 1998).
[20] Ervin Laszlo. *Science and the Akashic Field.* (2004).

Depression and World War 2 several years before they happened.

When questioned in this state he was also able to clarify and give details on past events, such as creation, the origin of humans, several events recorded in the Bible, the pyramids and the Ancient Egyptians, and specific details about varying cultures and popular figures in world government past, present, and future. Many of which unfolded after his death and are still being revealed today. Over the course of his career many famous world leaders and entertainers such as Harry Houdini, Thomas Edison, Woodrow Wilson, FDR, and Marilyn Monroe visited him.

During the height of his popularity he was, of course, accused of being a quack and demonic. Being a lover of God and faithful to his beliefs he loved helping others more than anything and was hurt by these allegations. Especially from his fellow Christians and those in the medical field. This often caused him to question what was happening to him.

Being very close to his mother, he always confided in her about his fears and insecurities, and she was typically the one who reminded him of his experience with the apparition, of his prayer of helping others, and that he should remain faithful. She also told him, "Everybody takes it for granted even the best Christians, the ministers, and missionaries that the things that happened in the days of the Bible and the days of the saints can't happen now."

Among many, one highly notable healing was that of his wife, Gertrude. She had been diagnosed by local physicians with a fatal form of Tuberculosis. Before turning to her husband for help, doctors had informed Gertrude Cayce that her tuberculosis was severe and that her prognosis was very poor.

They suggested that her condition was serious enough that she might not survive more than a few more months.

These conventional doctors had recommended that she undergo a long and arduous treatment that involved surgery. Specifically, they wanted to remove several ribs to help collapse her lung. This was a common treatment for tuberculosis at the time, known as *thoracoplasty*, which was meant to give the infected lung a chance to rest and heal.

However, this procedure was highly invasive, risky, and offered no guarantee of success. Many who had followed this course of treatment still did not survive. If she did live through the surgery, there would be a long recovery period with significant pain. Multiple physicians had confirmed her condition, giving her the same prognosis.

Faced with this grim prospect, Gertrude was hesitant and deeply afraid to move forward with the doctor's recommendations. She had, up until then, been quietly skeptical of her husband's gift. She loved him very much, but a Christian herself, she was just as uncertain as some of the others. However, facing her mortality and feeling there was no alternative she turned to him for treatment. Cayce, consumed with the fear of losing his wife, had already known that he was only able to help someone if they complied, so when she asked, he quickly arranged the reading.

Below I have written some specifics of the treatment plan given to Gertrude in the reading. The treatment involved several components, primarily focusing on natural remedies and lifestyle adjustments. Here are the key elements of the treatment:

1. Inhalation of Fumes: Inhaling the fumes from a combination of ingredients, including creosote and other substances,

which were heated to create vapors. These fumes were meant to cleanse and disinfect her lungs.

2. Poultices: Castor oil packs applied directly to the chest. This was meant to soothe the lungs, reduce inflammation, and draw out impurities.

3. Diet: She was prescribed a very specific diet, one that was rich in nutrients to build her body's strength and immunity. The diet included easily digestible foods, mainly fruits, vegetables, and herbs to restore her overall health.

4. Osteopathic Manipulation: Regular osteopathic adjustments were recommended to ensure proper circulation and nerve functioning, which he believed would aid in the healing process.

5. Mental and Spiritual Support: The importance of a positive mental and spiritual attitude for healing was stressed. Prayer, meditation, and faith were strongly encouraged, which were integral parts of this healing philosophy.

This blend of natural remedies, nutritional guidance, and spiritual encouragement formed the foundation of all treatments, each accompanied by a specific time frame. Remarkably, every patient who faithfully followed the instructions reported complete recovery. Gertrude was 23 years old when she received her fatal diagnosis from doctors and like the others she also fully recovered. Despite their dire prognosis giving her only a few months to live, she lived for another 34 years.

In 1923, Cayce was approached by Dr. Wesley Ketchum, who had heard about him from several of his patients who were suddenly getting better after working with Cayce. Unlike Dr. Layne, Dr. Ketchum was an established and licensed physician, but like many other physicians who shunned Cayce, Ketchum was also a cynic. However, he was more curious and open to understanding how he could better help his patients, so he paid Cayce a visit. After having his own reading and being healed he too began working closely with Cayce.

Ketchum became an integral part of the practice as it continued to grow, supporting Cayce and taking on the role that Dr. Layne had played, freeing Layne to pursue proper licensure. Ketchum, like the others, was impressed by the accuracy of Cayce's readings and wanted to understand the nature of his abilities from a scientific perspective. He suggested having Cayce undergo a medical examination at a university where he could be professionally evaluated while in trance. He hoped that it might lend credibility to Cayce's work within the medical community.

Having been mistreated by so many doctors over the years, Cayce was initially hesitant. However, his desire to help others and his trust in Dr. Ketchum led him to agree to the examination. His only condition was that Ketchum ensured his protection while he was in the trance.

The examination was arranged at the University of Cincinnati, where Cayce and Dr. Ketchum were joined by a group of university affiliated doctors and medical professionals who agreed to observe and evaluate Cayce while in his trance state. Those who attended had already heard about Cayce, and some of the professionals present approached the meeting with skepticism intending to disprove Cayce's abilities as legitimate. However, all were interested in understanding Cayce's process, particularly his ability to accurately diagnose without schooling.

During the evaluation, Cayce provided detailed medical diagnoses and treatment suggestions for specific cases presented to him by the attending physicians. Those present were reportedly impressed by the accuracy and depth of the information, primarily since Cayce had no training and was not consciously aware of the details he conveyed during the readings. This session helped legitimize Cayce's work among some members of the medical community, although skepticism remained among most of them.

The Examination Process:

The doctors and professionals who were in attendance closely monitored Cayce as he lay down and relaxed into a self-induced sleep-like state. The doctors then submitted several test cases, including medical conditions of patients that Cayce had no prior knowledge of. These cases were designed to test his ability to diagnose and recommend treatments accurately. Cayce's responses were documented carefully as he provided specific diagnoses, descriptions of physical conditions, and suggested treatments using precise medical terminology.

Even so, some of the doctors remained openly skeptic and condescending towards Cayce, viewing him as a curiosity rather than a serious subject of study. In effort to "expose" him as a "fraud" some doctors deliberately asked irrelevant or inappropriate questions, which demonstrated their intent to ridicule rather than genuinely assess his abilities. At least one account suggests that some of the physicians laughed and made sarcastic remarks during the session, showing a lack of professionalism. The behavior of these doctors was seen by some as unethical and unnecessarily cruel. Cayce, still in the trance, remained unresponsive to the erroneous questions.

To test the claim that he was completely unaware of physical sensations while in this altered state some of the more skeptical doctors performed provocative experiments. These included inflicting physical harm with sharp objects, such as needles or pins, to poke or stab Cayce in various parts of his body, expecting him to flinch or show signs of discomfort. When this did not happen, one of them took the blade of a knife and inserted it deep into the heel of his foot. Again, he remained motionless, further adding to their intrigue and confusion, but confirming his assertion that he was not consciously present during the readings.

Despite the unethical and downright rude behavior of some attendees, Cayce's accuracy in diagnosing, his knowledge in prescribing effective treatments, and his lack of response to stimuli stunned them all. While the session won over a few skeptics, others remained unconvinced, attributing his accuracy to coincidence or other non-paranormal explanations.

When Cayce came out of the trance, he was not immediately aware of what had transpired during the session and had no memory of what he said. However, when the discomfort from the poking and stabbing set in, he was visibly in pain. This upset his wife, and she did not hesitate to express her anger with Dr. Ketchum. She felt he did not follow through with his promise of ensuring Cayce's safety.

Cayce himself, while characteristically calm and non-confrontational, reportedly shared his wife's concern about the lack of respect and care shown during the session. He trusted those around him to safeguard his well-being while he was in the trance state, and the incident underscored how vital it was for someone to advocate for him during sessions. From then on, his wife took on the role of his primary protector during the readings.

The Cayce readings taught that Christ Consciousness is the ultimate spiritual ideal, encompassing qualities like love, compassion, forgiveness, and unity. This state is also a profound healing force, capable of restoring balance not only to the body but also to the soul. Healing, in Cayce's view, is a natural outcome of aligning with divine energy, though it often appears miraculous to others. He believed that by striving for spiritual attunement, individuals could access similar healing power, manifesting peace, love, health, and wholeness in their own lives.

As I continued exploring the many paths to spiritual growth and alignment, one truth became increasingly undeniable: deep, lasting, transformative healing requires more than just treating symptoms. It demands a return to wholeness. This realization is what led me to the remarkable work of Edgar Cayce. In my view, his legacy bridges science, spirit, and the sacred. [21]

"Very truly I tell you, whoever believes in me will do the works I have been doing, and they will do even greater things than these..." −John 14:12

---

[21] This chapter draws primarily on the life and work of Edgar Cayce as presented in Thomas Sugrue's *There Is a River*, Sidney D. Kirkpatrick's *Edgar Cayce: An American Prophet*, and materials published by the Association for Research and Enlightenment (A.R.E.). The interpretations, commentary, and spiritual insights offered here are the author's own unless otherwise noted.

SOPHIA C. RUSSELL

12 Rediscovering God's Medicine

"The day science begins to study non-physical phenomena; it will make more progress in one decade than in all the previous centuries of its existence." —Nikola Tesla

As discussed in the prior chapter, Cayce's readings offer more than curious metaphysical insight. They offer practical, God-centered guidance on how to heal the body by honoring the mind and spirit. In this chapter, we'll examine how his approach not only challenged the medical establishment but also echoed a divine truth long known by prophets, sages, and ancient healers: healing comes from within, and God has already provided the tools.

In today's society, we are a people who have been programmed in two important and profound ways when it comes to our physical health. #1 We trust that our established medical professionals make every effort possible to help us heal from discomfort and disease, and #2 Our Western Medical establishment is the best possible way of addressing illness and disease. I should add #3 We are also somehow persuaded to believe that natural methods don't work.

Holistic treatment is from God, and it works when carried out correctly.

We literally put our lives in the hands of physicians, trusting (blindly) that these professionals are studying all possible avenues of healing and providing us with the highest level of care. All the while continuously researching and enhancing their knowledge and skillset. Each physician is required to take and adhere to the Hippocratic oath which includes, among other vows, the following:

Prioritize patients.
Put the health and well-being of patients first and consider their autonomy and dignity.

Practice with integrity.
Practice medicine with honesty, compassion, and humility, and avoid letting personal factors influence care.

Be a lifelong learner.
Recognize the limits of your knowledge and continue to learn and improve throughout your career.

Do no harm.
Avoid causing harm to patients and prescribe treatments that are beneficial.

I point these out to show how the physicians in Cayce's case and in thousands of others bypass these ethical guidelines when it comes to understanding phenomena worthy of much more thorough research. So what if it seems ridiculous, confusing, or strange? If a healer is in fact curing diseases, of which they claim have no cure, why are they being penalized?

Sidebar: Dr. Sebi – Healing Through Nature

Born Alfredo D. Bowman (1933-2016) Dr. Sebi was a Honduran engineer, herbalist, and natural healer known for promoting a plant-based, alkaline diet as a path to health and disease prevention. In the 1980s, he gained national attention after being taken to court in New York for practicing medicine without a license. In a landmark case, Dr. Sebi was asked to present evidence that his natural methods had cured people of conditions considered incurable by conventional medicine, including AIDS, cancer, and diabetes. He reportedly brought over 70 affidavits and testimonies from individuals claiming they had been healed.

These documents included medical diagnoses from licensed physicians prior to treatment with Dr. Sebi, as well as follow-up records from those same or other doctors confirming that the illness or disease was no longer present after following his treatment plan. While a few patients gave testimony on the stand, many others who had benefited from his treatment filled the courtroom in support.

The prosecution included representatives from the New York State Attorney General's Office and several medical experts, who challenged the validity of Dr. Sebi's claims and his right to treat people without a medical license. In his defense Dr. Sebi reportedly stated, "I give people natural herbs from the Earth, and they get better. But the physician gives them artificial drugs that cause harmful side effects, and I'm the one being called the violator?"

Despite being challenged by these professionals who held several years of formal education and established medical practices, the court ultimately ruled in Dr. Sebi's favor, allowing him to continue his work. Dr. Sebi's treatments are rooted in African and Indigenous healing traditions, emphasizing detoxification, electric foods, and returning to nature for wellness, principles that also align with the information in the Cayce readings. [22] [23] [24]

---

[22] "Dr. Sebi: *Eat to Live*." YouTube. (Nov. 2013).

[23] "*Dr. Sebi talks about his Supreme Court Case.*" (2015).

[24] Jamison. *"Herbalist Found Not Guilty in 'Fake' Healing Case."* (1988).

Over the course of Cayce's and Sebi's lives, they each established well-documented scientific evidence that the method and treatments they recommended worked and healed very serious life-threatening ailments, which many are still suffering from today. However, these stories are only found if one is searching.

Western medicinal practice as a whole generate and spend billions of dollars researching to create more drugs that address symptoms, not cures. While we, the people are led to believe we will be helped by these pharmaceuticals with all of their unnatural and dangerous side effects. And at the same time, we are persuaded to believe that herbal and holistic methods are ridiculous, unreliable, or don't work.

Western medicine tends to focus on the primary physical problem, cut it out, or use drugs to suppress the painful symptoms it causes. There is little discussion between doctor and patient about interpersonal relationships, lifestyle, spirit, or mental health. And these are crucial aspects to healing. The symptoms are how our bodies communicate with us, when they are suppressed we might feel better, but we have not addressed the cause. Thus, the body will go about finding another way to communicate, hence another ailment emerges.

When healing naturally, it's essential to commit fully to a holistic approach, one that integrates the mind and spirit alongside the body. Consistence in following the recommended treatment plan, for the full duration suggested by the healer, is critical. While natural healing methods are profoundly healthier, they demand greater personal discipline, deeper faith, and more time.

When someone says, "I tried it and it didn't work," I'd bet my last dollar that one or more of these key elements—time commitment, self-work, or spiritual engagement was missing.

We live in a society that keeps our minds distracted by material pursuits. Because of this we are conditioned to convenience, where prepackaged and processed foods are the norm, shifting to a fresh, whole-foods lifestyle for an extended period can be difficult.

Even more challenging is being radically honest with ourselves, acknowledging our faults, learning from them, and doing the deep work of change. And for those who've only known God through religion, the journey of healing the spirit can feel unfamiliar or even daunting.

Only in recent years has it even been recognized by Western Medical researchers that merely addressing the ailment physically does not bring true and lasting healing. Around 1977, what is called the Biopsychosocial Model (BPS) was first conceptualized by Dr. George Engel and Dr. John Romano. [25]

Engel and Romano's method suggests that to understand and properly treat a person's medical condition, one must also consider the patients' biological, psychological, and social factors. It is a more person-centered approach that considers the whole person and what factors in their lifestyle might be contributing to their illness.

The BPS model is based on the idea that these three factors are interconnected and that their interplay determines the cause, manifestation, and resolution of illness. Though this is an evidence-based approach available to any physician, there are very few who actually adhere to the model.

---

[25] Engel and Romano. *"The Need for a New Medical Model: A Challenge for Biomedicine."* (1977).

The BPS approach aligns with what both Sebi taught and Cayce expressed while in trance and what many other holistic healers, shamans, and native medicine men/women have asserted throughout generations. Disease and its healing are an interplay of the mind, the body, and the spirit.

Mind

- The lens through which I interpret reality — shaped by thought, belief, memory, and perception.
- It is the bridge between spirit and body, where intention is formed and free will is exercised.

Body

- The sacred vessel through which I experience the physical plane.
- It is nourished by the energy I consume, the actions I take, and the vibrations I carry.
- It reflects the alignment (or misalignment) of mind and spirit.

Spirit

- My eternal essence — the divine spark that connects me to the Infinite Creator.
- It links me to my higher self and the greater web of life.
- It is the source of love, purpose, and the remembrance of who I truly am.

While most, even devoted Christians, primarily rely on western medicine, the Bible supports the use of natural treatments. And God has placed them abundantly in the Earth to support our health and well-being. If medical science used even a small portion of the billions spent in creating more artificial drugs, to develop medicinal plant medicines instead, many more people would benefit.

However, we cannot place blame on the medical establishment for the way we neglect our own health and self-care. Many of us have the tendency to place our lives in the doctors' hands, expecting them to heal us after years of mistreating ourselves. When really the individual has the responsibility to work on their own mind, body, and spirit. The doctor should be a guide not a god.

In the book of Isaiah chapter 38, we find the story of King Hezekiah, who became gravely ill and through tears pleaded with the Lord to spare his life. Moved by Hezekiah's change of mind and spirit, the Lord granted him an extension of life, Isaiah then gave the remedy to cure the physical ailment, "Isaiah had said, Prepare a poultice of figs and apply it to the boil, and he will recover (Isaiah 38:21)."

"Fruit trees of all kinds will grow on both banks of the river. Their leaves will not wither, nor will their fruit fail. Every month they will bear fruit because the water from the sanctuary flows to them. Their fruit will serve as food and their leaves for healing (Ezekiel 47:12)."

"Then God said, I give you every seed-bearing plant on the face of the whole earth and every tree that has fruit with seed in it. They will be yours for food. And to all the beasts of the earth and all the birds in the sky and all the creatures that move along the ground—everything that has the breath of life in it—I give every green plant for food (Genesis 1:29)."

"Daniel then said to the guard whom the chief official had appointed over Daniel, Hananiah, Mishael and Azariah, 'Please test your servants for ten days: Give us nothing but vegetables to eat and water to drink. Then compare our appearance with that of the young men who eat the royal food and treat your servants in accordance with what you see.' So he agreed to this and tested them for ten days. At the end of the ten days, they were healthier and better nourished than any of the young men who ate the royal food (Daniel 1:11-15)."

"…On each side of the river stood the tree of life, bearing twelve crops of fruit, yielding its fruit every month. And the leaves of the tree are for the healing of the nations (Revelations 22:2)."

Let me clarify here that I am not at all against Western medical practices as a whole. I do not have to tell you how many people are aided every day by caring medical professionals who take on the honorable role of serving others tirelessly. However, we would need them less, if we understood more about the God within us and the medicinal plants that are growing all over the planet.

I want to bring you, my reader, back to yourself. You are the operant power (not the blame) for any event, trial, or circumstance in your life. When you first connect with your divine guidance through consistent meditation and prayer, renew and transform your mind by examining your thoughts and beliefs with honesty, compassion, and openness, and finally prioritize the proper care and maintenance of your body, you can address any ailment you face.

13 The Reinterpretation of Gods and Biblical Beings

"By faith we understand that the universe was formed at God's command, so that what is seen was not made out of what was visible." —Hebrews 11:3

The above passage clearly discloses that there is an active realm of existence ***unseen*** to the human eye, contributing to our material or ***visible*** world.

Although we currently exist in a three-dimensional (3D) reality, there are strong theories suggesting the existence of many other dimensions beyond our own. We understand 1D and 2D because we exist in 3D and can perceive dimensions beneath us. However, physicist and best-selling author Dr. Michio Kaku offers a compelling metaphor from quantum theory to help us imagine dimensions beyond our own.

He asks us to consider a fish living in a pond. The fish moves freely in its watery environment, but it experiences life only in two dimensions. Its perception is limited to what exists within the plane of its pond—it has no concept of "up" or "down" as we know it. The fish is physically bound to its 2D existence and cannot even imagine a third dimension. Yet that doesn't mean 3D space doesn't exist—it simply lies beyond the fish's perception.[26]

Now imagine lifting the fish out of the water. Suddenly, it sees an entirely new world—trees, sky, depth—realities it never could have conceived from within the pond. Another dimension, another way of existing. In the same way, our

---

[26] Michio Kaku. Hyperspace and a Theory of Everything. (2025).

inability to see or grasp higher dimensions does not mean they don't exist; it only reveals the limitations of our current perception.

There is intelligent life living in higher dimensions of reality, who have further advanced technology, and who can *pierce the veil* between us so to speak. When they reach out to us it can be alarming, but it is sort of like lifting us out of the water. Remember the old saying, "Just because you have not seen a million dollars does not mean it doesn't exist."

In truth there are thousands, some accounts say millions of people around the world, who have interacted with life outside of this planet, currently and throughout time. Yet despite the thousands upon thousands of contemporary credible accounts of reported UFO and UAP (Unidentified Aerial Phenomena) sightings and experiences,[27] there are also numerous accounts in the Bible where beings from somewhere other than Earth either visited here or communicated with, or through a person.

Though the scribes of the Bible (the people writing the account) gave these beings names that coincided with their beliefs, calling them "angels, gods, Lord, or God," these visitors can be viewed without the lens of religion. Without this filter, they were just beings who were not from Earth and paying a visit.

Sidebar: The Rise of the Ancient Astronaut Theory

The Ancient Astronaut Theory proposes that advanced extraterrestrial beings visited Earth in the remote past and directly influenced early human civilizations. According to this view, many myths, religious texts, and unexplained

---

[27] *Unacknowledged: An Exposé of the World's Greatest Secret.* (2017).

architectural feats are not just symbolic but literal records of contact with non-human intelligence.

While speculative ideas about "star people" and divine visitors have existed for centuries, the theory became widely known in the modern era starting in the 1960's. About this time, Swiss author Erich von Däniken published Chariots of the Gods.[28] His book argued that ancient structures like the Egyptian pyramids, Stonehenge, and the Nazca Lines were built, or inspired, with help from advanced beings mistaken for gods.

This idea was further expanded in the 1970s by Zecharia Sitchin, whose Earth Chronicles book series presented translated Sumerian texts describing a race of celestial beings said to have created humans through genetic engineering.[29]

Since then, the theory has evolved into a global phenomenon, especially through the Ancient Aliens TV series launched in 2009.[30] Though mainstream academia remains skeptical, the theory continues to inspire curiosity, debate, and a rethinking of humanity's origins.

IF you pay close attention, there are numerous scriptures in the Bible acknowledging people's worship of other gods. The writings chosen by the church councils to make up the Holy Bible are written from the viewpoint of one god, capitalizing the "G" claiming the God of "Heaven" and the God of Abraham, Isaac, and Jacob to be *the one true* God. However, I wonder if the councils had instead collected the writings about Baal or some other god, and put them out in mass production, would the world be worshipping differently today?

---

[28] von Däniken, *Chariots of the Gods? Unsolved Mysteries of the Past.* (1970).
[29] Zecharia Sitchin. The Earth Chronicles. 7 vols. (1976–2007).
[30] *Ancient Aliens.* Kevin Burns and Giorgio A. Tsoukalas. (2009–present).

The Mesopotamians, such as the Akkadians and Babylonians, called their moon god *Sin* [31](Suen in Akkadian, Nanna in Sumerian). In our version of the Bible the word *sin* is used as a defiance of God's laws and references certain behaviors as a "sin" which is derived from the German word "syn" meaning *offense*. So for example, if I believe that my God (the God of Abraham, Isaac, and Jacob) is the one true God, and you are worshipping another one, in this case a god named "Sin" then I would view you as wrong.

However, there is an error within this frame of thinking, the One God, which I also call, Source *is* everything, therefore no one is "wrong" in this way. We have been grossly miseducated to believe that God is outside of us, and so we are always looking outward for evidence, guidance, support, and answers. *Stay with me.*

In the original Greek texts of scripture, the word often translated as "sin" is *hamartia*. A term that literally means "to miss the mark." Rather than implying wickedness or moral depravity, *hamartia* more accurately conveys the idea of a mistake, error, or failure to reach one's intended purpose. In classic Greek, it even referred to *a tragic flaw or human shortcoming*, not necessarily a moral offense. *Hamartia* (or sin) does not refer to overt evil acts, but to a condition of missing the intended design for human behavior and spiritual alignment.[32]

Understanding this shifts how we view our missteps. When I fail, make a mistake, or my actions lead to harm, I'm not committing an offense against a distant, external God. Rather, I am acting in a way that is out of alignment with God

---

[31]"Nanna/Suen." The Open Richly Annotated Cuneiform Corpus (ORACC), University of Pennsylvania

[32] Mounce. *Mounce's Complete Expository Dictionary of Old and New Testament Words.* (2006).

inside of me—the inner Source. I can usually recognize this misalignment by how I feel afterward: through emotions like guilt, regret, shame, unease, or disconnection, which signal that I've stepped away from my own inner truth. I've missed my intended mark.

This concept is reflected in Romans 3:23, which says, "For all have sinned (or hamarton, from hamartia) and fall short of the glory of God." The verse emphasizes falling short, not in the sense of condemnation, but in missing alignment with my divine nature.

If God is everything, then who was the God of Abraham, Isaac, and Jacob, and the many other gods mentioned in the Bible and ancient texts?

Today, the world is divided into seven continents containing nearly 200 countries, each with its own rich history and ancient writings. Across these diverse cultures, including the Egyptians, Greeks, Mayans, Inka, as well as other various African, Chinese, Indian, Japanese, European, Mexican, and in Indigenous populations throughout the world, recurring themes appear in their earliest belief systems and religious texts. One striking commonality is the presence of sky beings, often described as powerful figures who descended from the heavens and were revered as gods. Yet despite these global parallels, mainstream academics largely dismiss these accounts as mere mythology.

In ancient Rome, another name used for Earth was "Terra" and the word "terrestrial" is from Latin "terrestris" meaning, *of or belonging to the Earth.* The word "extra-terrestrial" only means *from outside the earth or its atmosphere.* With this clarified definition we can view ourselves as terrestrial, and these visitors from the sky as "extraterrestrial" or ET.

Although most people don't typically think of angels, gods, or divine beings as extraterrestrials, they are by definition, not from Earth, and therefore qualify as ETs. It's largely due to societal conditioning that we fail to see them this way. Popular media, especially movies and television, have shaped our perceptions with frightening depictions of ETs as a dangerous threat, fueling fear around the idea of intelligent life beyond Earth. However today, this concept shouldn't feel so far-fetched. With initiatives like SpaceX actively planning to colonize Mars, it's entirely plausible to consider that advanced civilizations elsewhere have already achieved such feats.

Among the many researchers who explore the hidden history of humanity and our contact with other worldly beings, author and speaker David Icke stands out for his bold and thought-provoking interpretations. In his book "The Biggest Secret" Icke challenges readers to reconsider traditional religious narratives, particularly those found in the Bible, not as purely spiritual allegories, but as literal accounts of extraterrestrial visitation. He writes, "Wherever you read in the Bible of angels, lords, gods, etc., replace it with extraterrestrials and you will have a very good idea of how long we have been being visited." [33]

Let's take a more pragmatic look at a few of the instances recorded in scripture.

"I looked, and I saw a windstorm coming out of the north, an immense cloud with flashing lightning and surrounded by brilliant light. The center of the fire looked like glowing metal, and in the fire were what looked like four living creatures. In

---

[33] Icke. *The Biggest Secret: The Book That Will Change the World.* 2nd ed., (1998).

appearance their form was human, but each of them had four faces and four wings (Ezekial 1:4-6)."

Here we have the prophet Ezekial explaining a personal experience he had with a craft coming out of the sky. Throughout the book, he gives a detailed description of not only the craft but also the beings inside, calling them "creatures." Theologians explain Ezekial's experience in many ways, but by just reading it yourself without their interpretation, it becomes evident this is a close encounter.

"When human beings began to increase in number on the Earth and daughters were born to them, the sons of God saw that the daughters of humans were beautiful, and they married any of them they chose (Genesis 1:1-2)."

"The Nephilim were on the earth in those days, and also afterward, when the sons of God went to the daughters of humans and had children by them (Genesis 1:4)."

In these passages the writer makes a distinction between humans and the "sons of God." These *sons of God* were clearly not humans themselves or the distinction between them and the humans would not have been noted. The writer also notes that these *sons of God* were mating with human women who bore their children. This means these *sons of God* were sexual beings and able to procreate with humans. If these were in fact divine beings (i.e. angels, fallen angels, or demons) as some theologians teach, why would they desire sex and reproduction?

The passage also gives us another name "The Nephilim" who the Bible notes were *on the Earth* in those days. Where are they now? According to Sitchin (and others who follow the ancient astronaut theory) *the Nephilim* were another name for the extraterrestrials (the *Watchers*) who mated with human women. Among various theories in theology, one is that the Nephilim are the offspring of *fallen angels* and human women, another is that these were mythical giants or warriors whose presence reflected the growing corruption of pre-flood humanity. Despite what might actually be the truth, it is evident that these were not Earth humans. [34] [35]

Sidebar: "Because of the Angels"

Some religions require women to wear specialized loose clothing that covers their entire body or at minimum head coverings, often explained as cultural or moral traditions. But an ancient, lesser-known reason may be hidden in 1 Corinthians 11:10, where Paul writes: "It is for this reason that a woman ought to have authority over her own head, because of the angels."

This cryptic passage has sparked debate for centuries. Some interpret it as a reference to the "sons of God" in Genesis, beings who lusted after human women. The coverings, then, were not just about modesty, but protection, a way for women to shield their curves from these entities and maintain control over their own bodies. As we see in the Genesis 1 passage these beings "married any of them they chose," leading me to believe that these women may not have always consented.

The verse in Corinthians feels abruptly cut off, hinting that something deeper may have been left out. Possibly something that points to ancient interactions between humans and otherworldly beings.

---

[34] Sitchin. The 12th Planet (2007).
[35] Roberts. *The Rise and Fall of the Nephilim: The Untold Story of Fallen Angels, Giants on the Earth, and Their Extraterrestrial Origins.* (2012).

"After six days Jesus took with him Peter, James, and John the brother of James, and led them up a high mountain by themselves. There he was transfigured before them. His face shone like the sun, and his clothes became as white as light. Just then there appeared before them Moses and Elijah, talking with Jesus (Matthew 17:1-3)."

The above quote from the Bible is entitled "The Transfiguration" and appears in the books of Matthew, Mark, and Luke. Oddly, it is not recorded in the books of the eyewitnesses, John, James, or Peter, but has been given to us by people who were not there. So, we only have the story from those who heard about it. If the eyewitnesses wrote an account, we don't have it. Perhaps their firsthand accounts ended up on the editing room floor when the Bible was being put together. Why the council decided to include second and third hand accounts instead, we will never know.

Again, let's remove the religious filter to give us a clearer view. After all, during this time there was no belief system called "Christianity."

Imagine that you are an eyewitness, and are hanging out with this man who is teaching about God, healing people, restoring sight, etc. You wake up and witness, to your amazement, two beings just appear and are now standing before you. Their bodies are so illuminated that it is difficult to describe.

You also see the spiritual teacher you have been following around listening to everyday, transfigure into this same body of light. He is speaking to the two beings, who in human or Earthly terms had died long ago. However, they are alive and standing before you also in their energetic light bodies. The three have a discussion and are then enveloped into a "large cloud." Upon the lifting of the cloud, there is only your teacher there, and back in his Earthly or fleshly body. Where did the other two beings appear from and where did they go? Heaven? Where is that?

In Genesis 11, The Tower of Babel, "But the Lord came down to see the city and the tower the people were building. The Lord said, 'If as one people speaking the same language they have begun to do this, then nothing they plan to do will be impossible for them." Come, let us go down and confuse their language so they will not understand each other.'"

Here, "the Lord" or being, seemed surprised by the unity of the people and their accomplishments. The being also says, "let *US* go down." Now why would God (The ultimate Creator of all, who is all knowing) be surprised at human unity, then sabotage it? And who are the "us" he was speaking to?

When I first read the account of the tower I was confused. Because personally, I thought it was pretty awesome that this community of people were so united that they were able to work together successfully towards a common goal. However, theology tells us that this act by the humans was blasphemous and arrogant. That these people were instituting their own power in response to the flood to provide themselves protection from another deluge, and to become known as a powerful city.

I searched through my Bible repeatedly to find support for these theories but could not. I found online that this explanation is found in other historical accounts which are not included in the Bible. This gave me great pause, because I thought that I did not have access to these other historical accounts to come to my own understanding, so I figured I was left to take the word of the theologian.

However, the Sumerian tablets, which predate biblical scripture by at least a thousand years, and in some cases much more, offer a detailed account of the tower narrative. In *The Earth Chronicles* (the series of books based on Sitchin's translation of the original tablets) he presents extensively researched interpretations of Sumerian history. Sitchin's work is regarded by many as one of the most comprehensive attempts to decode this vast body of ancient texts.

According to these accounts, the structure commonly referred to as the *Tower of Babel* was not merely a symbolic monument, but a launch tower intended for space travel. The tablets explain that the humans were constructing it to ascend to the skies just as the "gods" had done, possibly as a means of escaping another cataclysmic flood.

However, factions of these "gods," also described as advanced interstellar beings, opposed humanity's access to space and broader cosmic knowledge, thus they halted the construction of the tower through the *confusion of languages*.

In the book of Genesis "God" says "Let US make man in OUR image…" In its original Hebrew text, the word used for God here was "Elohim" which is plural meaning "gods" telling us that there was more than one being present. The singular word for God in Hebrew is *Eloah* but this was not the word used by the initial scribe. However, it was translated for us from plural to singular, "God."

Another passage we find reflecting multiple "gods" is found in Psalm 82:1 "God has taken his place in the divine council; in the midst of the gods he holds judgment." This powerful passage used the word *Elohim* for both God and the other *gods*, showing a heavenly council or divine assembly that includes multiple beings called gods.

This switch up in translation may never be known by the average believer, but it is known by Biblical scholars. The primary theological theory is that it was the man we call Jesus there with God, but this is speculation by theologians to explain it because of the passage in John 8:58 where Jesus said "Before Abraham was, I am." However, when you understand the "I Am" as God as everything or All That Is, this passage is not support that this was the man we call Jesus with God in Genesis.

We're often presented with the Book of Genesis as a comprehensive account of the beginning of everything. In reality, it offers a simplified overview, focused specifically on the formation of Earth and the emergence of modern humanity on this planet only. It does not address the creation of the broader universe, other planets, or the potential existence of life and civilizations elsewhere in the cosmos. Because most people are introduced to this story at such an early age, few ever pause to consider what's not included in the text.

What is included are elementary depictions of historical events, intertwined with allegory and metaphor intended to convey spiritual truths and moral lessons. Take the story of Noah, for instance. He was instructed by a being or "god" to build an ark in preparation for a massive flood. He was also told to bring aboard two of every animal species, a task that, on the surface, seems logistically impossible.

This has led some modern thinkers to speculate: What if Noah wasn't preserving live animals at all? What if he was safeguarding genetic material, an ancient form of DNA to repopulate life on Earth after the flood? While this isn't a traditional theory, it reflects a broader interest in re-examining ancient texts through a modern lens that includes technology, biology, and cosmic awareness, three areas obviously experienced by ancient humans.

The Bible teaches that Noah was chosen because he was "righteous," but earlier texts, such as those found in the Book of Enoch and certain Mesopotamian writings, suggest a deeper, more controversial reason. In these accounts, Noah was born of a mixed bloodline, the child of a human woman and a celestial being. His father, one of the "gods" also known as the "watchers," wanted to save his own offspring from the destruction the other Elohim planned, keeping his bloodline active on the Earth.

In 1 Enoch 106–107 the story tells how Lamech, Noah's father, becomes disturbed because his newborn son looks unusual, his face was shining like the sun, his eyes were glowing, and he could speak right away. Lamech says, "I have begotten a strange son, diverse from and unlike man, and resembling the sons of the God of heaven."

In Genesis 18 & 19 "the angels" came down and visited Lot and ultimately destroyed the cities of Sodom & Gomorrah. Though they are described as *angels*, in reading the passage you will see that they ate, and slept (verses 3-4), and in verse 10 and 12 they are referred to as "men." Why would divine beings need food and rest?

Additionally, Mary, Joseph, and Elizabeth, the mother of John the Baptist, each received visitations, and there are numerous other accounts of beings appearing from "the skies." Prophets speaking of future events, and priests or teachers retreating into tents or secluded spaces to commune with "God" before delivering the messages they received to the people. Theology has found ways of explaining away our commonsense understanding when scripture is clear. And this is easy for them to do because of our fear of intelligent life outside of Earth.

There are two prominent figures in the Bible, Elijah, and Enoch whom the scriptures say were *taken*. Though the scribes say they were "taken by God," upon reading we see that they were taken by visitors from outside of Earth. It is likely that the scribes, seeing these beings through the lens of religion and having no other way of understanding how they maneuver, called them "God" because the experience seemed miraculous.

After all, if you were walking along the street and say a "chariot of fire" suddenly appeared before you and the friend you were walking with was swept up into the sky in a "whirlwind" (2 Kings 2:11), not having any understanding of what this moving vehicle was or how it could actually fly, you too may attribute the event to a divine being.

One book that was initially included but later removed from the Bible is the book of Enoch. This is especially curious since the Bible mentions him favorably in Genesis. "Enoch walked faithfully with God; then he was no more, because God took him away (Genesis 5:24)." It does not say he dies, but that he was taken. Today we still hear of people being "taken" but instead we call it *abducted*. At the time of my writing, there are free PDF versions of The Books of Enoch available to download online and I have provided a link on the reference page.

"And, while I slept, a great distress entered my heart, and I was weeping with my eyes in a dream. And I could not figure out what this distress might be, |nor| what might be happening to me. Then two huge men appeared to me, the likes of which I had never seen on Earth. Their faces were like the shining sun; their eyes were like burning lamps; from their mouths fire was coming forth; their clothing was various singing; their wings were more glistening than gold; their hands were whiter than snow. And they stood at the head of my bed and called me

by my name. Then I awake from my sleep, and saw those men, standing in front of me, in actuality. Then I bowed down to them; and I was terrified; and the appearance of my face was changed because of fear. Then those men said to me, 'Be brave, Enoch! In truth, do not fear." [36]

In his writings Enoch describes in detail being taken into the "heavens" and what he experienced with the beings while traveling the skies. Biblical scholars state that his writings were removed because they are inconsistent with the teachings. However, we know that Enoch lived and that he was faithful, so though not necessary, it might be a good idea to read what this prophet had to say.

When speaking to those in my prior church community regarding the many writings that are not included in today's Bible, I often got the answer that they are not canonized. While I was a practicing Christian, I just said, "ok." However, when I started to do more research, it dawned on me that I did not have a full understanding of what that meant. I realized it had something to do with being approved, but then I thought, "Well, who is doing the approving? And why am I allowing them to approve things for me?"

According to Webster's Dictionary, the word *canonize* means *to officially recognize something as part of a rule or standard.* In the context of the Bible, canonization refers to the process by which early church leaders decided which writings were considered sacred or inspired by God. As discussed in Chapter 6, this was not a single event but a gradual process that unfolded over several centuries and by hundreds of councils.

---

[36] *2 Enoch,* Chapter 33 (sometimes numbered as Chapter 32 in alternate versions), verses 2–8

The Roman Catholic Church played the central role in shaping the biblical canon, especially in the Western world. Councils such as the Council of Hippo (393 AD) and the Council of Carthage (397 and 419 AD) all led by Catholic bishops, were instrumental in finalizing which books would be included. These decisions, later reaffirmed by the Council of Trent in 1546, established the structure of the Bible most commonly used today, including books that some later Protestant traditions would exclude. [37] [38]

In short, canonization was the process of formal approval by early Catholic Church councils, through which the foundational texts of the Christian Bible were assembled and affirmed.

As a young woman who had spent over 20 years as a devout Christian, who did not consider herself a Catholic, I was shocked to find that I had been subject to the censorship of Roman Catholic leadership. This is about when I learned the benefit of meditation, and I started to build a stronger connection with my own inner guidance.

I have learned to trust that God, who dwells in me, will guide me to more and more understanding as I seek. "Then you will call on me and come and pray to me, and I will listen to you. You will seek me and find me when you seek me with all your heart. I will be found by you, declares the Lord, and I will bring you back from captivity (Jeremiah 29:13)."

When we truly seek God, answers unfold. However, many confuse *seeking God* with joining an organized religion,

---

[37] Metzger. *The Canon of the New Testament: Its Origin, Development, and Significance.* (1987).

[38] Tanner. editor. *Decrees of the Ecumenical Councils*, Vol. 2: Trent to Vatican II. (1990).

reading the Bible, or going to church more. These would be seeking to be more religious, not more spiritual or Godly.

For many, being part of a church or spiritual community can be a meaningful and helpful part of their journey, and I am not saying that there is anything inherently wrong with that. However, it is not a commandment or law from God, but rather an encouragement found in the New Testament (Hebrews 10:25). Having a supportive social network of friends and associates is beneficial because when we come together in love, our collective energetic frequency raises and we all feel supported. However, it is wise to navigate how we do that at our own discretion, using our own inner guidance. Again, when we tell others what they *must* do, we infringe upon the free will that our Source allows.

SOPHIA C. RUSSELL

14 Sacred Frequencies: The Language of Spirit

*"What we call God **is** Consciousness. The energetic Source of **all** that exists; masculine and feminine, animal and plant, mineral and chemical, positive and negative, physical and nonphysical." —Me*

Let's briefly take a more in-depth look at channeling as it relates to the more accepted terms of direct revelation or prophesying. These are related concepts that involve receiving and conveying messages or guidance from a source believed to be beyond the ordinary human realm. When one is operating through a religious belief system, they fully accept the idea that a person can receive messages from a divine being and convey it to others.

In addition to the passages shared earlier, this is also evidenced by the apostle Paul, who by his own claim said he was stopped and spoken to by a long-departed Jesus while traveling along the road. His story was corroborated by Ananias, who also claimed to be visited by Jesus and told to go to Paul (Acts 9).

Today, however, if I were to tell you that I was stopped on the road and received a message from a being or source beyond this dimension, most people aren't so quick to accept it. Strangely, it's often easier to believe such experiences when they're written in ancient texts or spoken by figures from thousands of years ago. But when it's someone living today—perhaps someone standing right in front of us—our openness tends to shift.

We saw this with Edgar Cayce, and we continue to see it with modern-day channels and messengers. Instead of curiosity or respect, they are often met with doubt, skepticism, or even ridicule, especially by those who are very committed to their religion.

This dynamic was also present during the lifetimes of Paul and the man we call Jesus. While they attracted many devoted believers, the majority of people, especially those rooted in the traditional religious systems, did not accept their teachings and this pattern continues today.

If the man we call Jesus is to return as taught in Christianity, it is likely that today's church goers would not recognize him at all, nor would he recognize them as his students. Matthew 17 states, "Many will say to me on that day, 'Lord! Lord! Didn't we prophesy in your name? Didn't we drive out demons in your name? Didn't we do many miracles in your name?' Then I will tell them clearly, 'I never knew you.'"

What the man we call Jesus taught was not mainstream; it was a radical, alternative spiritual path that challenged the established order, and very few churches today teach what he did.

The interpretation given in contemporary churches does not reflect this teacher's original message. Their traditions and way of life differ greatly from what he lived and taught. What I mean is, much of what we know today as Christianity would be equivalent to the established religious order of the Pharisees described in scripture.

And while some of you might be saying, "not my church." I get it, because when I was an active member, I would say the same thing. Then proceed to list off all of the wonderful acts of service we were involved in, how we strove to be loving, and treat people with respect and equality in the name of Jesus. And I am so grateful for the commitment I was called to there.

Because without it, I don't know that I would have studied my Bible like I did, which led me to actually seeing all the discrepancies that I am bringing your attention to.

When those early church councils gathered together all of those thousands of times, they essentially worked to organize a religion, something the man we call Jesus did not take part in while alive. They adopted and institutionalized his movement; and the original teachings were restructured to serve political and imperial agendas. What began as a mystical and personal path of spiritual awakening was transformed into a formal religion: Christianity. Today, it is the world's largest faith tradition, with approximately 31% of the global population claiming the faith, that's about 2.4 billion people.

But large numbers do not guarantee truth. As the cover of this book reflects, we are warned in Matthew 7:13–14

"Enter through the narrow gate. For wide is the gate and broad is the road that leads to destruction, and many enter through it. But small is the gate and narrow the road that leads to life, and only a few find it."

This verse reminds us that the popular path is likely not the enlightened one. Simply identifying as Christian (or not) doesn't determine one's spiritual maturity or salvation. What ultimately matters is our vibration, the frequency of energy we emit through our thoughts, emotions, intentions, and actions. This energetic signature is what aligns us with either higher divine consciousness or lower realms of being. Energy, vibration, attraction, and frequency are not topics traditional Christian churches discuss at all.

Your vibration emanates from you and aligns you with the people, circumstances, and events that match that frequency, you are doing this nonstop despite your religion. This is why you will often see devoted Christians who are also angry, judgmental, anxious, poor, sick and/or depressed. While someone who claims no belief system at all might be kind hearted, happy, abundant, healthy, and at peace. It is not the religion or your worship of an external God that determines your attunement with Source, it is your inner alignment.

Every one of us has the innate ability to receive insight and guidance from beyond the physical realm. This intuitive connection is a natural part of our spiritual design. Yet, throughout history, certain individuals have been more attuned to this flow, those we often refer to as prophets. The very reason they were given that title was because of their heightened ability to channel information from interdimensional sources and deliver messages that carried wisdom, warning, or inspiration.

FEAR – False Evidence Appearing Real

But while this capacity exists within us all, most people struggle to access it fully. Why? One of the greatest barriers is fear. Fear interrupts the natural transmission of higher knowledge. It creates static in our spiritual signal. Doubt, anxiety, and cultural conditioning all reinforce the idea that we are separate, unworthy, or incapable of such connection. Over time, this disconnection becomes normalized, and what should be an everyday, divine dialogue is treated as rare or even impossible.

Fear doesn't always show up as outright terror, it often masks itself as doubt, self-judgment, or a belief that spiritual gifts are reserved for "special" people. Many of us have been conditioned, often through religious teachings, to view anything beyond the physical as dangerous or deceptive unless it comes through an officially sanctioned source. As a result, we become afraid of our own power, afraid of hearing, seeing, or knowing too much. We question whether our experiences are real or worry about being labeled as strange, unholy, or delusional.

In these subtle yet powerful ways, fear serves as the line between the conscious self and the higher self. It reinforces the idea that we are small, separate, and dependent on intermediaries to connect with the divine. But the truth is that this connection has never been broken, it has only been quieted.

To reclaim it, we must begin to recognize when fear is speaking louder than truth. Practices like meditation, journaling, breathwork, and spending time in nature help clear the energetic clutter. Trust builds slowly, but the more we listen and respond to the subtle nudges from within, the stronger that connection becomes. This is not about becoming a prophet or a channel in the traditional sense; it's about becoming fully aligned with your own inner knowing.

Media also plays a powerful role in shaping our fear-based reactions to things we don't fully understand. Through television, films, and sensational storytelling, we're often conditioned to associate the unseen or unknown with evil.

It's not just media or religion, however, perhaps a personal experience that felt overwhelming or frightening can also cause us to shut down spiritually and avoid anything that reminds us of that event. This is understandable and if you dig deeper, it happens with many things we don't comprehend.

Consider the fear you had before learning to drive or swim. Anytime someone invited you out, all kinds of horrific thoughts and images may have popped into your head, and rightly so, but this does not mean they are all valid. Anyone can go out and swim, but it is their own belief that makes that possible for them or not.

Before I learned to swim, I was terrified of going into deep water. I mean I would physically shake and was even too scared to drop tears. One day when I was a young girl, my father put me on his back, swam out into the deep end of the pool, pushed me off, and then called for me to swim back to him. After having done this, I have loved swimming ever since.

Typically, when I have discussed channeling with people who are religious, their first reaction is a warning, "You better be careful. There are entities out there you don't want to fool with." The more religious they are, the more fearful they are of something evil happening. I would think it to be the opposite. That the commitment to the religion would bring more confidence in God's protection, but this is rarely the case. At the same time, I understand, because as stated, I felt a little fear myself before gaining more knowledge of the channeling process and our own innate abilities.

In my experience, I found that while the church teaches that God is all knowing and powerful, it also instills this incredible fear of a devil into us at the same time. So, while I am claiming, if God is with me, who can be against me (Romans 8:31)? I am not necessarily living that way, because I am also taught that the devil is prowling around looking for someone to devour (1 Peter 5:8). We are constantly confronted with double talk and wondering if we are doing something against or displeasing to God.

Through my personal study and experience, I have found that there are also very loving, giving, and caring entities out there, who love God, and want to help us know what has been kept from us. Many are like family and care about our well-being. Like my father, they know we can swim and want to help us learn how.

Let me just note here that I only have these discussions with people who want to know. I do not argue or try to prove things (*anymore*) with those who are set in their belief system. I have learned that each of us has come into this Earth plane with a certain lifestyle we wished to explore, and some have come with the purpose of experiencing a religious one. So, it would be intrusive of me to try and change that. (We will discuss life plans more in a bit).

However, there are also those of us who love God, and only chose our religion because we were taught that it was the only way to be close to or to serve God. This belief is another result of miseducation. We serve God simply by *being,* and once we come to be, we cannot stop being. Nope, not even by suicide.

"Humans come to earth to "BE" not to "do." When humans master who they have come to BE, all the doors will open up for what they would like to do and have. Humans must BE first." −Angel Guidance as channeled by Jamillah Shabazz

Sidebar: Unpacking Resistance to Channeling

If the idea of channeling brings up discomfort or resistance, it's worth taking a moment to explore where those feelings come from. Often, what we reject isn't the practice itself but the beliefs we've inherited around it. The questions below are designed to help you uncover your own understanding, whether you're skeptical, curious, or simply seeking clarity. Even if channeling isn't a personal concern, these reflections may help you support others who are asking similar questions.

Reflective Questions:

- *Why do I believe that God spoke through people like the prophets in ancient times—but not through anyone today?*

- *Why do I assume that the individuals who translated ancient texts always had pure intentions and never made mistakes?*

- *Why do I feel uneasy, or dismissive, when someone says they channel messages now?*

- *Why do I find it harder to trust a living person I can see, hear, and question, than a historical figure I've never met?*

Take your time. Write your responses honestly. Notice what you discover.

In general, the word channel is defined as a *path that leads from a source to an outlet.* We also use this word in discussing water flow and electrical currents. In truth we are all channels, we receive information from Source and use it in our everyday lives all the time. One obvious way is how our bodies work. What medical science calls our autonomic system; how you are breathing, how your heart is pumping, when you cut yourself and it heals, and so on. We are all constantly channeling from Source. Think about that for just a minute before moving on.

However here, we are discussing individuals who have learned to fine tune this ability to use it in a specific manner. By this definition, the prophet is also a channel, it is just that the prophet is conveying messages through the filter of their religion and naming a known personality within it. The channel on the other hand is not using this filter, they are allowing the pure message of the being to come through and sharing it with others, without the restriction of a religion, as given in the example of Cayce.

One reason we are comfortable with the prophets in scripture is because we have become so familiar with the personalities in the Bible, it seems like we know them intimately. It is much the same with celebrities. We have seen, heard, and admired their work for so long that we grow to trust their word. This is why they can sell us products we may not have bought without their endorsement.

However, we do not really know them, we only feel like we do because of familiarity through repeated exposure. Now, when a channel brings through an individual who is living in another realm or reality and we have never heard of them, it is very difficult to trust who it is.

That being said, asking how to navigate between safe and unsafe conditions when contacting other realms of reality is a good question. I have found that learning how to take precautions when venturing into other dimensions is good to do. As spiritual beings it is important to walk in the assurance that **God Is All That Is** and has given us the ability to navigate ourselves safely.

The cosmos is filled with intelligent life, and just like here on Earth, some beings are benevolent while others are not so much. While there are beings aligned with peace and spiritual evolution, others operate from lower vibrations and self-interest. What determines which energies we attract? Again, it all comes down to the frequency we are emitting. Through the Universal Law of Vibration and the Law of Attraction. These laws are aligned with *Free Will*; we resonate with whatever matches our energetic frequency.

Remember, the Universe responds to your frequency, which is shaped by your genuine thoughts and emotions. You can't deceive the Universe the way you might fool others. In essence, the vibration you carry attracts the experiences and energies you encounter. When you stay aligned with Source, your frequency becomes a compass, guiding your journey. But if your focus shifts toward fear, the Universe will mirror that as well, it always responds to the energy you project.

Let's say you are on a long drive from one state to another. You take a turn into a community unfamiliar to you. By looking around, you immediately start to assess your surroundings and begin to feel either ok, or unsafe. Based on your feelings you make a choice to either remain in the area or find the first road out. The point here is that the decision is yours. You are the operant power, no being can infringe upon you, unless you give permission.

All That Is (God) has given each one of us intelligence and intuition, when we learn to use them properly, we can protect ourselves. It is when we don't use or ignore these innate abilities, that trouble could arise.

People who use their ability to channel are not willy nilly. They nurture the talent, knowing how and when it is wise to use it. If they enter onto a plane of existence and feel unsafe, they can exit. This understanding will guide you, even away from those who claim to be channels but are committing fraud or have negative intentions. "Submit yourselves, then, to God. Resist the devil, and he will flee from you." James 4:7

While I am providing background information about how channeling *works* to some degree, I am writing only for informational purposes and this is not a comprehensive instructional text. If channeling or any other practice discussed in this book is of interest to you, please seek guidance from a professional in the field. There are many practitioners who offer books and courses to get you on your way.

While both channeling and prophesying are similar, there are key differences in the ways these terms are understood and used across various spiritual and religious contexts. I have broken it down further, for more understanding.

Similarities:

•Receiving Divine Messages: Both channeling and prophesying involve the reception of messages or insights from a source considered to be divine, spiritual, or beyond the ordinary human capacity.
•Acting as Intermediaries: Practitioners of channeling and prophets are seen as intermediaries between the divine realm and humanity. They convey messages or prophecies that are believed to originate from a higher source.
•Spiritual Guidance: In both channeling and prophesying, the aim is often to provide spiritual guidance, wisdom, or insights that can be beneficial for individuals or communities.

Differences:

Nature of the Source:

•Channeling: In channeling the source of the messages can vary widely. It might involve communication with spirit guides, angels, ascended masters, extraterrestrial beings, or higher consciousness. The sources can be diverse, and the nature of the information received may cover a broad range of topics.

•Prophesying: Prophets, in many religious traditions, are typically seen as receiving messages directly from God or a supreme deity. The source is often singular and associated with the specific religious tradition in which the prophet operates.

Form of Communication:

Channeling: Channels may use various methods, such as meditation, trance states, automatic writing, or direct verbal communication, to receive and convey messages from another realm or reality.
Prophesying: Prophets, in many cases, receive their messages through visions, dreams, or direct communication with the divine. The manner of communication often aligns with the specific religious and cultural context.

Role in Religious Tradition:

Channeling: Channeling is often associated with New Age, spiritual, or esoteric movements. It may not always be recognized or accepted within mainstream religious traditions.
Prophesying: Prophets are often integral to the religious narratives of certain traditions, especially in Abrahamic religions like Judaism, Christianity, and Islam. Prophets hold a specific role within the established religious structures and scriptures.

Frequency and Purpose:

Channeling: Can be a more frequent and ongoing practice Individuals may channel regularly and for various purposes, including personal growth, healing, or providing guidance to others.
Prophesying: Prophetic messages are often depicted as occurring at specific moments in history or in response to

particular circumstances. Prophecies may have a more event-driven or episodic nature.

In summary, while both channeling and prophesying involve the transmission of messages from a higher source, the differences lie in the nature of that source, the methods of communication, their roles in religious traditions, and the frequency or manner in which these practices occur.

Throughout this book I am using channeled material to discuss information that I was never able to find while active in church. Though we have already touched on the life of Edgar Cayce, he is not rare. There have been thousands of teachers like him throughout history and still today. I have included a short glossary of a few contemporary channels in the back of this book and how to find them online. I will also discuss a few more of them as I continue.

15 The Power of Divine Imagination

"Imagination is the very gateway of reality. Man, through his imaginal activity, creates his reality." —Neville Goddard

We are all capable of finding our way just fine without ever consciously interacting with beings in other dimensions. However, there is something wonderful to gain when gleaning information from teachers who have knowledge beyond our current understanding.

Over the last ten plus years I have studied much of the contemporary channeled material, their books, videos, and the channels themselves. Though I now understand far more about creation than I did when I began this journey, I recognize that there will always be vast realms of knowledge beyond our reach.

Some of this is due to the inherent limitations of the time/space framework we are living in called a dimension. Some is because we are attempting to articulate realities that exist beyond the bounds of language itself. And some truths remain hidden simply because we chose to veil them from ourselves, for the joy of remembering, the thrill of rediscovery, and the beauty of unfolding understanding, what we might also call "living." With that in mind, I offer what I've come to know, as clearly and sincerely as I can.

The Seth Material, in my view, is one of the most informative and clearly discernable writings on the unseen world. This is a series of books that document the insights and philosophy conveyed by a consciousness, Seth, who was channeled through the co-author Jane Roberts, during trance states. Seth described himself as an energy personality essence who is no longer focused in physical reality. He claimed to originate from a non-physical spiritual realm and stated that he no longer exists in a traditional physical form.

Among many topics, Seth discusses the concept of each person including himself, having lived many lives. And that all the lives of an individual are lived simultaneously, but that it is our perception of time that creates the illusion of sequential past, present, and future. He teaches that each life we live contributes to the overall development and expansion of our soul's consciousness, and in turn this growth contributes to the expansion of God.

According to Seth, our existence is much like television programming. For example, you may be watching one channel or network, such as Hulu, and at any given time, you choose to watch one show on that network, let's say it's called "The Orville." Simultaneously, however, other programs are still running on other networks. It is just that you are tuned into (or focused on) one network and one program.

Living is a lot like this. Your consciousness is focused on this earth life (or network) and on who you are in this life (one program). Let's call this program a personality, and just like television programs are named to distinguish them from one another, you have given your personality a name, such as Sophia, Bobby, Denice, or Jose. However, you, as an over soul are much like The head of a large corporation, having the ability to run simultaneous networks (souls) and programs (lives).

Bear in mind that none of these "parts" (over soul, soul, and personality) are separate from one another; you, like the television set, are all of them working together. And just like the network itself is not a tangible object, meaning you can't reach out your hand and touch Hulu, so it is with your consciousness. You only know what Hulu is because of the receiver we call the television. Your physical body is the receiver, like the TV, and if the TV stops working or dies, Hulu does not and neither does your consciousness.

Referring to what I shared earlier about our perception of time, it is not the same everywhere in the universe. Just like we are able to call around the world and it be a different time but the same moment, there are conscious intelligent beings, physical and non-physical, which to us may exist in the future or past, but it is still the present moment.

Some may have lived lives on Earth and through what we call death; their consciousness left their body but continues to be. This is how Moses and Elijah were able to visit with the man we call Jesus, as discussed earlier.

Dr. Brian Weiss, MD, is a distinguished psychiatrist and hypnotherapist who graduated from Columbia University and Yale Medical School and served as Chairman of Psychiatry at Mount Sinai Medical Center in Miami. His career took a transformative turn when a patient unresponsive to traditional treatments for anxiety and depression began recalling past-life experiences during hypnosis sessions. These revelations, which included vivid memories of birth, death, and the afterlife, challenged Weiss's mainstream medical perspective and led him to explore the therapeutic value of reincarnation memories.

He documented this profound journey in his best-selling book, "Many Lives, Many Masters," which has sold millions of copies worldwide. The book recounts how revisiting past lives helped his patient overcome deep-seated fears and sparked global interest in the connection between spirituality, healing, and psychology. Weiss urged mental health professionals to stay open to unconventional methods, prioritize patient healing, and consider the mind, body, and spirit as interconnected, with past-life memories offering potential pathways to profound emotional breakthroughs.[39]

Though I will cover more about the concept of what we call re-incarnation later in the book, I thought it was important to include a snapshot here, so that we have a little more understanding about personalities existing outside of our current dimension and time zone. (We will explore more about what we call death in a bit).

The sessions between Jane and Seth began in the early 1960s and continued until Jane's passing in 1984. The series of Seth books covers a wide range of topics, including consciousness, the nature of reality, before and after life, and the power of beliefs, and I will refer to it more throughout the rest of this text. [40] I urge you, however, to read them yourself, (and the other references I cite) as I am giving you a summarized version of my best understanding, and you will learn far more about what I share when you do your own study.

The Beginning of the Beginning

Seth states, "Some of this discussion is bound to be distorted, because I must explain it to you in terms of time as you understand it. So, I will speak, for your benefit, of some indescribably distant past in which these events occurred.[41]

Seth explained that Source realized itself in a state of *non-being* (not to be confused with nothingness), a condition of energy potentiality where Source held excitement and expectation of all probabilities and possibilities but was unable to manifest them. "This was a state of agony in which the powers

---

[39] Weiss. *Many Lives, Many Masters*. (1988).
[40] Roberts. *Seth Speaks: The Eternal Validity of the Soul*. (1972).
[41] Roberts. *The Seth Material*. Bantam Books. (1984).

of creativity and existence are known, but the ways of producing them were not."

Seth said that as far as he knew "this agonized search for state expression may represent the birth throes of All That Is," *God*. He explains that Source felt an intense desire to express all the ideas It created in Its thoughts, however, initially was unaware of the way to release it into being. Seth stated, "Within All That Is, therefore, the wish, desire, and expectation of creativity existed before all other actuality. The strength and vitality of these desires and expectations then became in your terms so insupportable that All That Is was driven to find a means to produce them."

Imagine for a moment that you want to be a dancer with all your heart. You envision the feeling of dance, the clothes touching your skin, the music vibrating through you. You feel the talent of all the greatest dancers you have ever seen pulsating within you, but you are unable to stand.

You have legs but the communication between your brain and your legs is blocked. Each moment you ponder how to solve this problem, so that you can live what you imagine. You can put in place here a talent you love and wish to express but cannot. Now magnify this feeling, because for our Source, the intensity of the impetus is what led to *being*.

Channeled information and many philosophers throughout history have expressed that everything began and continues through thought. The way we use our imagination, our thinking, is our creative power.

Our imagination produces images, which then manifests into the physical. We are the *image* of God. God at Its origin is nonphysical, the Source of infinite conscious intelligence. When It imagines, It creates and the images It produces manifests into physicality. That may be galaxies, stars, planets, flora, fauna, and beings like you and me. Because of this we are all connected with one another, never separate from Source, and always have access to Infinite Wisdom. Great people whom we call geniuses today have given us examples of this.

Albert Einstein is world renowned for his groundbreaking contributions to physics. Through what he called his "thought experiments" he developed revolutionary theories that changed the world. Einstein described these exercises as imaginative journeys into the realms of space, time, and the nature of the universe. One of his most famous thought experiments involved imagining himself riding alongside a beam of light, which ultimately led to the formulation of the theory of relativity.

Though he is well respected today, during his time of initial experimentation and early career he faced harsh resistance and criticism from those in the academic, scientific, and religious communities. [42]Those prominent in the field believed his "thought" methods were ridiculous and that his theories were unsubstantiated, he was forced to take odd jobs to earn a living.

In truth, young Einstein was introducing innovative ideas that disrupted the established scientific beliefs of his time. And let's face it, many "highly educated" individuals often resist having their perspectives challenged. It's not about whether the new information is supported by evidence; more often, the real struggle lies in admitting we may have been wrong. The ego mind, which thrives on certainty and identity, often

---

[42] Isaacson. *Einstein: His Life and Universe.* (2007).

perceives being wrong as a threat, making it incredibly difficult to embrace new truths, no matter how valid they may be.

Before I move on, I can't go without discussing another great man, Nicola Tesla, who also faced significant challenges during his lifetime. Known for his pioneering contributions to the field of electrical engineering, Tesla designed and produced some of the world's most incredible and useful inventions, including wireless communication, which he fully developed in the late 1800's. However, this technology was not utilized until recently, and he was basically unacknowledged by academia.

Tesla also described engaging in elaborate thought experiments where he entered a meditative like state and mentally envisioned his projects down to the most intricate details. Through imaginative thought, he said that he worked out any proposed problems before constructing the project physically. Following his visualization, Tesla transitioned to the construction phase of his inventions with remarkable precision. Rather than relying on extensive time periods of trial and error, he claimed that any problem he might encounter was resolved first in his imagination.

In his autobiography, Tesla explained that he would mentally build and test his devices, making improvements entirely in his mind before ever touching a tool.[43] Those who worked closely with him confirmed how rarely he needed to revise his designs once they were built.

To put this into perspective, Tesla's process was highly unusual and unique. Typically, the process of invention and production includes extended periods of experimentation, prototyping, and refining, often lasting months or even years.

---

[43] Nikola Tesla. *My Inventions: The Autobiography of Nikola Tesla.* (1995).

Tesla's method stands as a striking testament to the power of focused thought, creative visualization, and mental discipline.

Tesla was also open about receiving information from outside of Earth and spoke of building devices to facilitate interplanetary communication. Considered an eccentric by colleagues and peers, he faced great opposition and skepticism from both the scientific and financial communities, which included men like Thomas Edison and J.P. Morgan.

In 1901, Tesla constructed a wireless power transmission station, the Wardenclyffe Tower, which he built to transmit electrical energy over great distances without wires. Tesla understood how to harness the abundance of natural energy present in the Earth's atmosphere in a way that can provide humanity with clean and unlimited free power. The cost of implementing his discovery is infinitesimal and far safer than the harsh and dangerous way our society continues to produce energy and fuel today.

When J.P. Morgan, who was funding his project, learned that Tesla was producing energy that would be freely accessible to the public **at no cost**, he pulled out his financial support, and the tower station was never completed. Still today we go on using destructive methods to process fuel and energy, and though it could be, these resources are not made available for free.

I could name others, but we can see in just these two men that when we learn how to use our imagination properly, we have access to unlimited knowledge and information. Yes, they went to school, but each of them credits their connection with the unseen as the primary source of their knowledge rather than their educational experience. The institution only served as an outlet for them to express and enhance their innate talent. Though we may not aspire to impact humanity as incredibly as they did, we at minimum hold the power to create a better lived experience for ourselves.

In English imagination is defined as *the production of sensations, feelings, and thoughts associated with images.* We tend to use this word interchangeably with "make believe" or "pretending" as if imagining means something that is not real. YOU were first imagined before you became physical. Imagining, pretending, and even "make believe" are necessary precursors to all manifestation. Nothing in all creation is done without it. Let's break it down a little more.

I-MAGI-NATION

Perhaps some readers may recognize the word "Magi" right away, which many religions (especially Christianity) refer to simply as "wise men." However, the term Magi has deeper historical and cultural meaning. Originating from the Old Persian word *magus*, the plural *Magi* referred to a priestly class, known for their expertise in astronomy, astrology, dream interpretation, and sacred rites.

These men were indeed wise, yes, but this was largely due to the fact that they were trained in what was then seen as mystical or esoteric sciences or again, *universal laws.* So, while modern religious narratives often simplify the Magi as wise travelers, various ancient texts portray them as powerful initiates, trained in cosmic principles and deeply attuned to metaphysical knowledge. What this really means is that their training in universal laws expands beyond what the average population understands.

In our history, Egypt functioned as an intellectual and spiritual epicenter of the ancient world, where much of this training took place. Comparable to today's Ivy League institutions, Ancient Egypt was not just a center of religious practice, but a hub of deep metaphysical study and was renowned for its training in mastery of universal laws. Numerous legendary teachers, scholars, and messengers including the man we call Jesus, along with Pythagoras, Plato, and even Moses were trained in Ancient Egypt.

Seekers of knowledge were often initiated into Mystery Schools such as those at Heliopolis, Abydos, and the Temple of Luxor, where spiritual training was considered a sacred science. These schools taught disciplines like sacred geometry, astronomy, alchemy, and holistic healing, along with deep studies of universal laws and consciousness. Some esoteric scholars suggest that today's concept of calling an advanced school of study a *university* was derived from these ancient centers of learning.[44] [45]

While today's colleges tend to emphasize logic, empirical science, and material knowledge, the original universities were focused on awakening the whole person, mind, body, and spirit, through self-knowledge, inner alignment, and cosmic or *universal* understanding.

When an individual knows how to access and use these universal laws, it looks like a miracle or "magic" to us. Which is what we see in the Magi, the lives of the prophets, in the man we call Jesus, and in quite a few other spiritual teachers throughout history. Understanding how to align the power of God within themselves, (which is in all of us) they were able to execute acts that appear miraculous to those of us who do not know the laws.

---

[44] Manly P Hall. *The Secret Teachings of All Ages* (1928).
[45] Schwaller de Lubicz. *The Temple of Man: Apet of the South at Luxor* (1998).

In John 14:12, the man we call Jesus declares, "Very truly I tell you, whoever believes in me will do the works I have been doing, and they will do even greater things than these..." Yet, this powerful promise is rarely embraced fully by those who claim to follow him. In many churches, this passage is either overlooked or spiritualized into abstraction, rather than taken as a call to actual potential.

Most followers today struggle to believe they could truly do the works he did, and it is this disbelief that keeps them from experiencing it. As we see in Matthew 13:58, even Jesus was limited in what he could do among those who lacked faith: *"And he did not do many miracles there because of their unbelief."* This suggests that it is not simply divine will but also our belief (or the lack thereof) that determines what is possible.

Additionally, when people do express this power, we might dismiss it, ridicule them, declare it as evil, or in some cases worship them as a god, as with the man we call Jesus. So much so that we are trained in many churches that we ***must*** pray to God ***in*** Jesus's name, or that our salvation is ***only*** possible ***through*** Jesus. What?

Consider this, today we know a little more about technology than people say, 300 years ago. If you were to hop into your little time machine and travel back to the year 1700 and show the people a laptop, a cell phone, or better yet make your landing in a 747, the people would be awestricken. As you exit the vehicle they may even bow and call you God. An airplane is so outside of what they understand to be possible, it would appear miraculous. You, however, know that it is not a miracle or magic, it is simply the manifestation of advanced thinking.

This is likely why many visitors to Earth in scripture and throughout our world's ancient history were called gods, lords,

141

or angels. These beings did not challenge the title, because they understand God as everything, therefore they see themselves as divine and also equal to you and me.

However, the Earth human has been programmed away from this knowing, and so we are limited in our capabilities and experiences by being given a reality that we are taught to believe. This is the meaning of Psalms 82:6-7, "I said, 'You are gods; you are all sons of the Most High.' But you will die like mere mortals; you will fall like every other ruler."

The lower case "g" refers to all beings who come out of Source (God) but as discussed earlier, still have the power of the Source within them. You are also a god; it is only that you have not been trained in the laws of the universe. You have been programmed to believe that you are a "mere mortal." And the programming is so effective that to believe you hold the power that creates planets within yourself sounds ridiculous.

In the movie The Truman Show, actor Ed Harris plays Christoff the creator and executive producer of the show. In one scene a reporter questions him, "Christof, let me ask you, why do you think that Truman has never come close to discovering the true nature of his world until now? Christof replied, "We accept the reality of the world with which we're presented. It's as simple as that."

Sidebar: From Thoughts to Things

Everything that exists began as a thought in someone's imagination, a chair, a house, a business, a career, a marriage, a child, even an airplane. Before any of these took form, they were first conceived in the mind. Take a moment to ponder this.

Let's continue defining our word "imagination." The word *nation* refers to a large body of people united by a common thread, while the letter "I" symbolizes the divine presence within you, the God within. When broken down, imagination can be understood as *I am a nation of magicians.*

This reflects a deeper truth: we are each creators, made in the image of God, endowed with the power to shape reality, unified and connected into One. Whether we realize it or not, we are constantly crafting our lived experiences through the energy of our thoughts and the focus of our inner vision.

If we don't like what we are experiencing, we must change our thinking. We have been taught to "see it to believe it" when in truth we must believe it *before* we will see it. The mental is 100% always before the physical. Hebrews 11:3 tells us that "what is seen was not made out of what was visible."

Michael Jackson, one of the most iconic artists in entertainment history, often spoke about the power of intention and belief. Long before the release of Thriller, he would affirm to himself daily that he would create the biggest-selling album of all time.

He stated, *"I look in the mirror, and I would say it over and over to myself. I'd take a deep breath, put my feet together, raise myself erect, strong like a hero warrior, and I'd say, 'Biggest-selling album of all time, greatest seller,' over and over in my mind, and look into my eyes. And I'd mean it. I'd say, 'Biggest-selling album of all time.' And I wouldn't accept anything unless this was exactly what I wanted. My attitude was: I want the biggest-selling album of all times, to break records, to do phenomenal work."* [46]

---

[46] *"Michael Jackson's Personal Affirmations Helped Him Make Thriller the Biggest Selling Album of All Time."* (2024).

He wrote the affirmation on sticky notes and placed them all over his home, especially on his mirrors, so he would see them constantly. This was not just wishful thinking, it was a deliberate spiritual practice of aligning his mind and spirit with a vision he was committed to manifesting. His faith in the unseen, paired with inspired work and creativity, ultimately led to *Thriller*, which still holds the record today (40+ years since its release and nearly 20 years after his passing) as the best-selling album of all time.

You may be thinking, "Well of course, he's Michael Jackson. Easy peasy," but it wasn't that cut and dry.

Though the Jacksons had unquestionable fame during their career, in the mid 1970's the group was in a slump, concert ticket and record sales were declining. And if you don't already know, large record labels have no problem cutting their losses and focusing their funds onto newer younger artists.

Michael, being the standout star for so long, was being encouraged by his team to go solo before the group's ultimate ending. He had started his visualization and intention practice before working on his first solo album, *Off the Wall*, and wholeheartedly believed that it would be the album to break the record.

Though Off The Wall went on to receive numerous awards and accolades, including a Grammy and 9x Platinum certification, it was not the outcome Michael had visualized. Though most artists would be over the moon with its success, Michael was disappointed and tested the Universe. He reportedly stated that it was his frustration around the outcome of

Off the Wall that motivated him to work smarter on Thriller.[47] [48]

This story is a powerful reminder that our words and thoughts are tools of creation. Michael's method echoes ancient metaphysical truths: what we repeatedly focus on, we draw into our lives. By impressing his subconscious mind with a clear, bold vision, he opened a pathway for divine inspiration and human action to meet. This practice is available to all of us. Whether we're building a career, healing from trauma, or seeking spiritual growth, consistent affirmations aligned with belief and inspired action can transform our inner landscape, and eventually our outer reality.

If you do not like something about the reality you are living in, pay close attention to your thoughts for just 3 days and the feelings they produce in you. Take note without judgement of them, just pay attention.

Let's re-cap. Our thoughts produce feelings and because we are energetic beings, together (thoughts and feelings) create a frequency that goes out from us and draws back those events, circumstances, and people who match that frequency. God is not a man out in a distant realm blessing or cursing you. Source (God) is the invisible embodiment of law and allows us as part of itself the free will to utilize It at our discretion.

"Everything is energy and that's all there is to it. Match the frequency of the reality you want, and you cannot help but get that reality. It can be no other way. This is not philosophy. This is physics."–Bashar as channeled by Daryl Anka

---

[47] Taraborrelli. *Michael Jackson: The Magic, The Madness, The Whole Story.* (2009).
[48] *Thriller 40.* Directed by Nelson George. (2023).

SOPHIA C. RUSSELL

16 In the Beginning was the Thought

"For God does speak, now one way, now another, though no one perceives it. In a dream, in a vision of the night, when deep sleep falls on people as they slumber in their beds, he may speak in their ears..." —Job 33:14-16

One evening I was researching and in the note taking stage of preparing to write this book, I went to sleep with a question on my mind, as I often do. I have learned that in our sleeping state we have access to other realms of reality and through practice we can remember the experience and sometimes find answers.

While dozing off, I asked for more understanding about our connection to Source. While in my sleeping state, I saw a very dark planet sized sphere with hundreds of circuit like lanes going out from its center, and the center was a large golden glowing ball of light, somewhat like how we see the sun. The circuit lanes crossed over and around one another with little twinkling lights moving along them. I did not see it, but I felt a loving presence there with me, and I asked, "What are the little twinkling lights?"

I was telepathically told, these were living beings, coming out from Source, and moving along the lanes experiencing their lives. I asked, "Well what's outside the sphere?" and my view changed, it expanded upward and outward. I was being given an aerial view, like from an airplane, but the sphere kept expanding further and further out, going on to infinity, showing innumerable lanes and lights. This dream enhanced my understanding of our energetic reality, and I saw what represented Source releasing all of its creations from Itself, while remaining connected with everything.

According to Seth, All That Is searched within Itself for an answer to the dilemma it found in Itself. This strong focused desire gave birth to the solution, *letting go*. In that moment Source knew It would have to lose part of Itself (see Logos below) to free all of creation from thought to *being*. In so doing, Source is everything that we know in our universe, because everything springs out from It.

Seth explained that All That Is does not know of anything like Itself and It knows It sprang into Consciousness but does not recall *how*. From our human perspective, just as it is difficult for us to recall our own birth, perhaps this is so for God, or maybe it is just that in human terms it cannot be articulated.

A young man Matias De Stefano is another teacher who explains what he knows about the origin of the Source. De Stefano gives his audience a personal account as he still has full memory of his "past" lives, particularly experiences in ancient civilizations, and he shares his unique perspective of human and universal history.

In his show "Initiation" which airs on The Gaia Network,[49] De Stefano gives an account of the beginning of everything. He explains that we are all born remembering where we came from before being in this current life, but at around age three most people's minds begin to disengage from those memories and focus their full attention here in this life. However, De Stefano says he has never forgotten and remembers his other lives a lot like the way you and I remember important events from our childhood, but in a lot more detail.

---

[49] De Stefano. *Initiation*. Gaia, season 1, episodes 1, 2, and 5, aired 30 (2019).

According to De Stefano, the physical world was not created in a linear manner but rather through a process of energetic evolution and consciousness. He suggests that various cosmic energies, dimensions, and frequencies interact to give rise to the material realm through Gods thoughts. He calls God, Consciousness and says that everything is Consciousness.

In his view, everything seen and unseen *is* Consciousness experiencing Itself through Its creation. He says that Consciousness *is* Unity, and this is the first dimension in which everything exists. The first dimension is the Original Consciousness, and he also calls it the One Mind.

The thoughts going out or the thinking of Consciousness creates waves of sound (energy and vibration). I believe this aspect of Consciousness is what is called "Logos" (discussed more below), which gives way to everything else; space, time, all dimensions, realities, and whatever they contain. Unity is constant and was not created by Consciousness, Consciousness *is* Unity. It is the only thing there is, and we are all in It, and made up of It. We are all a projection of the One Mind.

De Stefano says that in the original beginning the first dimension, Consciousness only knew one thing, Itself. If we were to put it in our language, God knew "I Am." It then asked itself "Who can I become?" This was the Original Thought, and the beginning of everything else. According to De Stefano it is impossible to give the event a time because time does not exist in the first dimension.

When we receive new information, the brain instinctively tries to make sense of it by referencing what it already knows. However, this beginning defies our usual contexts of understanding, making comparison nearly impossible. To truly grasp the depth of these concepts, we must turn inward, because it is within that the answers reside, along with the capacity to comprehend them.

According to De Stefano the only way to perceive Unity is by using our imagination, we must forget or unlearn those convoluted manmade theories about what or who God is. When we sit in meditation and in silence, we will experience a sort of nothingness, the void, neutrality. Once this is achieved, we can begin to feel Unity. Consciousness, God, is felt, this is the first dimension that contains all, and feeling it is a way to know it more fully.

Over the years many have told me how difficult it is to meditate, that they cannot quiet their minds. I have found that most give up practicing before they ever reach this deeply connected state with the Divine. In this chaotic world we live in, our minds are easily distracted or occupied with those things we feel are important.

When we sit to meditate, any and everything can pop into our minds from family or relationship challenges to problems at work, issues with money, health, or even just needing to clean the bathroom. All sorts of thoughts start scurrying around.

As discussed in chapter 3 this mental chatter will continue its race around your mind until you discipline it, and meditation is a useful tool in calming it down. This is a practice that takes patience, quietness, and consistency. The person who desires to reap its benefits should be open and persistent. I often suggest starting with 5 minutes each morning and evening, building from there steadily overtime.

When we are active in religion many of us learn to pray rather than to meditate. It is not that meditation is not found in scripture; it is. (Genesis 24:63, Joshua 1:8, Philippians 4:8,

Psalms 1:2, Psalms 19:14, Psalms 49:3, Psalms 104:34, Psalms 119:15, Psalms 119:148, Psalms 143:5, Psalms 119:99, Psalms 77:10-12).

Nonetheless, not many traditional churches train or encourage meditation, or even speak of it very much. I think of prayer as asking mode, while meditation is receiving mode. The problem and the solution are on two different energetic frequencies, and if I remain in the frequency of the problem, I cannot match the frequency of the solution, leaving my prayer unanswered.

The Ra Material is another series of channeled messages also known as *The Law of One*.[50] This unified entity identified themselves as Ra, and said they are a non-physical collective intelligence in the 6th dimension. The project began in the early 1980s when Carla Rueckert, a channeler, started receiving communications from Ra through deep trance states. Don Elkins, a physicist, and Jim McCarty, a scribe, together with Carla, formed the core team responsible for documenting and disseminating the information learned from Ra.

Through Elkin's questioning, Ra explained that they visited Earth in physical form during the time of the ancient Egyptians. They said they had been watching and felt they could offer useful assistance in helping the people of that time in Egypt (or Kemet before it was renamed by the Greeks) to understand Creation and the Law of One. In book 2 of the series they describe themselves, "Our physical beings were what you call golden. We were tall and somewhat delicate. The covering of our physical body complex had a golden luster."

---

[50] Rueckert, Elkins, and McCarty. *The Ra Material: The Law of One*, Books 1–5. (1984–1998).

Ra stated, "We are old upon your planet and have served with varying degrees of success in transmitting the Law of One, of Unity, of Singleness to your peoples. We have walked your Earth. We have seen the faces of your peoples. We found it was not efficacious."

Ra explained that between the vast difference in their appearance and ours and their knowledge about such things as healing, technology, and consciousness, which they freely shared, the people began to worship them, which they did not want. Ra sees everyone in the universe as brothers and sisters. All are an equal part of the One Infinite Creator, and no one is over another. However, they found that the priests and the rulers distorted their message. The knowledge they shared was not distributed among all the people but was being reserved only for those in power. Once Ra realized this, they left.

According to the information from Ra, many races from throughout the cosmos have visited Earth going back millions of years. This teaching coincides with the information published by author and hypnotherapist Dolores Cannon where she expands on this idea stating that Earth has been visited by beings from all across the universe for millennia. She explains in her book *The Convoluted Universe* that these visitors did not just observe, they interacted with, guided, and many (not all) even interbred with early human populations. According to Cannon, these genetic influences help explain the vast diversity in human appearance, language, and cultural expression.[51]

Within the 5 book series, Ra also shares how many of the anomalous structures which were built in various locations all over the planet, to include the building of the pyramids, were

---

[51] Cannon. *The Convoluted Universe*: Book One. (2001).

done through thought. Which we might call levitation (this happens when one knows how to communicate with another type of consciousness. It can also be done through sound). This helped me to better understand the scripture in Matthew 17: 20, "Truly I tell you, if you have faith as small as a mustard seed, you can say to this mountain, 'Move from here to there,' and it will move."

Ra explained that their involvement in our remote past caused a chain reaction of unwanted consequences that they did not intend. Thus, in hopes of helping to reverse the impact of their initial presence, they have never stopped assisting humanity and those who are seeking *the Law of One*.

Ra calls God, "The One Infinite Creator" and the term "Logos" is used to represent the intelligence responsible for the creation of the universe. Ra suggests that the Logos, driven by a spontaneous desire for further self-awareness and exploration, initiated creation. This act of creation involved the Logos projecting aspects of itself out to manifest various dimensions and densities, resulting in the formation of galaxies, stars, planets, and all life forms, which all have consciousness.

This creation process is described as an ongoing exploration of the One Creator gaining experience through the innumerable manifestations of consciousness.[52] Everything is conscious, planets, air, water, rocks, and things considered to be inanimate. These are all *different* forms of consciousness, and they do not all communicate like the human consciousness, but they do all communicate. Because we are all part of the One Mind, through training, we can learn how to communicate with other types of consciousness, hence supporting this passage above in Matthew 17 as literal.

---

[52] https://www.llresearch.org/

153

This is why mainstream scholars cannot explain these structures; they neglect deeper study or acknowledgment of these universal laws. Even when the physical evidence is standing right in front of them over 400 feet tall.

According to Ra the relationship between The One Infinite Creator and the Logos is central in understanding the creation process. The One Infinite Creator is described as the ultimate, undifferentiated Source of all that is, an infinite intelligence or unity that precedes and transcends all manifestation. Logos, on the other hand, Ra states is a focal point of intelligent energy that initiates the process of creation.

Logos is considered a creative principle that serves as the interface between the formless unity of The One Infinite Creator and the manifestation of the universe. It is the intelligent energy or concept that brings forth the blueprint for creation, setting the stage for the formation of all manifestations.

In other words, the Logos function as a kind of architect or organizing principle that guides the evolution of consciousness within the created realms. It is associated with the Word, found in scripture and is the vibrational frequency that shapes the fabric of reality.

The Logos is not an entity in itself, but a principle or concept through which creation unfolds. Love is intricately intertwined with the Logos, serving as both the source and expression of the creative intelligence that governs the universe. This understanding of Love is beyond how we as humans typically define it, as it truly has NO conditions.

This is what I believe is being discussed in the Bible, John 1 "In the beginning was the Word, and the Word was with God, and the Word was God…" The Greek word for WORD is *Logos* and it is defined as *divine rationality. The principle of order and knowledge.*

John was likely referring to this process of energy or thoughts going out from God being manifested into everything else, just as words are the expression of thoughts. John is not referring to the Bible or the man we call Jesus. Remember our discussion earlier that one definition of 'word' is command. "By faith we understand that the universe was formed at God's command, so that what is seen was not made out of what was visible (Hebrews 11: 3)."

Depending upon your belief system, it may be difficult to understand God as Source Energy and still feel connected. Seth states, "but since its energy forges your person, how can this be?"[53] We are bombarded with what seem to be solid and real objects all around us, believing that we ourselves are physical. Never learning that we are always encased in an unseen, but vibrant energetic body, with a built-in emotional guidance system.

From our current perspective it is easier to see God as a man and outside of us in a distant realm, making human like judgments of our behaviors, but we came out of our Source and It is never separate from us.

Just like our Source, we are all made up of energy. Think about the electricity that is generated at a power plant. Using various processes, it is initially taken from the atmosphere, then transmitted through wires into our neighborhoods and homes where we can utilize it in any number of ways. The current itself becomes most useful when it is paired with a physical receiver, such as a bulb, TV, a computer, etc.

---

[53] Roberts. *Seth Speaks: The Eternal Validity of the Soul.* (1972).

When we turn on a switch, we expect the bulb to illuminate the room, and unless something has disrupted the current it will work properly. If it does not turn on, we know that the connection with the source has been interrupted, so we go about figuring out what the problem might be, i.e., loose or damaged wires, etc. However, we understand that the source (that is the electricity ever present in the atmosphere) is always available, but it is the connection with it that at some level needs to be repaired or adjusted for it to flow.

So what disrupts our energy's flow from Source?

According to Ra our body is a temporary vehicle for the soul's exploration. Scientifically speaking it is a grouping of cells vibrating at a phenomenal speed that appear solid (see chapter 7) . We use the body in our dimension as a receiver, and we always have a consistent flow of power from our Source coursing through us. This power is ours to harness and direct, allowing us to shape the lived experiences we most deeply desire.

However, our connection with Source can seemingly be blocked by our own thoughts and beliefs. I say "seemingly" because the power is always flowing, but because it follows the direction of our thoughts and beliefs (free will), we often direct it in ways we do not want, and in turn we repeatedly blame ourselves, others, or circumstances and events for our problems and find no resolution.

For example, you pray for money which is abundant on the Earth and available to everyone, but you *think* it is difficult to come by, that you are broke, and say it often which reinforces your belief. Thus, the flow of energy, at your command, will continue to produce the physical result of lack in your lived experience. This backwards and unconscious way of thinking is often the result of our upbringing, traumas, and life challenges, and we pass this mindset on through each generation.

Blockages, such as growing up in poverty, abuse, judgment, strife, dysfunction, and discord are thieves of a full abundant life. The Bible taught that these are hinderances (blocks) and to throw them off and run the race marked out for you. These blocks can only be removed by fixing our thoughts on "things above" gentleness, peace, patience, faith, love (Philippians 4:8).

Despite what it appears to be in the visible world around you, once you consistently replace your lower thoughts and belief patterns with higher ones, over time you will see the momentum of your thinking switch to a new and more desired direction, which will be followed by experiencing a more fulfilling life. (John 10:10, Hebrews 12:1, Galatians 5:22).

SOPHIA C. RUSSELL

17 Not in the Sky, but in You

"So we fix our eyes not on what is seen, but on what is unseen, since what is seen is temporary, but what is unseen is eternal." —2 Corinthians 4:18

We all grow up knowing our physical body has a time limit. When we finish with it, we discard it and continue living in our *energetic* (soul) state. This is the energetic body of Light that many of the beings visiting here appeared in as we noted earlier in the scriptures.

Seth proposed that the terms *All That Is* or *Source* might be a bit more fitting to identify God. However, he cautioned that whichever name you prefer to call God, do not view It as something separate and apart from you. The One God is *everything* yet invisible and is not out in the sky or residing in a distant spiritual realm in a human figure sitting on a throne. Though it cannot be seen with an eye or touched with a hand, it is seen in creation and felt in the heart.

"If you prefer to call the supreme psychic gestalt God, then you must not attempt to objectify him, for he is the nuclei of your cells and more intimate than your breath." [54]

"For in God we live and move and have our being (Acts 17:28)."

According to Seth, from Its agony Source found the way to burst forth into freedom, through expression, and in doing so it gave existence to all individuated consciousness. "Therefore, It is rightfully jubilant. All That Is loves all that It has

---

[54] Jane Roberts. *The Seth Material*. (2001, pp. 245–246).

created down to the least, and It is triumphant and joyful at each development taken by each consciousness."

Our Source, as it is within each of us, expands Itself by our experiences. Whether we see them as negative or positive, there is always expansion. Seth states that Source is highly attuned to you, directed, and focused within each individual, residing within each consciousness.

Each consciousness is therefore cherished and individually protected. "The coming of the kingdom is not something that can be observed. Nor will people say here it is or there it is because the kingdom of God is within you. (Luke 17:20-21)."

My husband never knew his father. His mother met him shortly after moving over a thousand miles away from her childhood home when she was only 18 years old. In her innocence she was swept away in a brief love affair with an older man and became pregnant. Unable to support the baby on her own, she moved back home with her family. She never even had a picture of his father.

My husband says that he was always able to talk openly with his mom and very curious, he often asked her what his father looked like. He said she always told him, "Boy, if you want to know what your father looks like, just go look in the mirror."

God is the unlimited, unbounded field of awareness that permeates all things (Greer, 2017). Conscious Intelligent Infinite Love Energy. It is you, and you are It. Still, there are no words to accurately convey all God is.

The BEST way to know what God is, is to look in the mirror. If in any way you perceive God as somewhere other than in your own wonderful being, or that the Bible is the only word of God, you have the wrong God and have been miseducated in your understanding of the Word.

"You are everything, every being, every emotion, every event, every situation. You are unity. You are infinity. You are love/light, light/love. You are. This is the Law of One." —Ra, as channeled by Carla Rueckert

18 Those Who Came from the Sky

"The gods of myth were not born of the Earth, but came from the heavens, riding fire and cloud." —Unknown

So far, I have given a VERY simplistic overview of the origin of God, creation and how we are all aspects of one Consciousness. We are all part of One Mind. I gave a little background education on the Bible and the many ways our Source always has and always will communicate with us. Next, I want to chat a little more about creation; visible and invisible, this includes dimensions, densities, physical and non-physical realms. But before moving forward, it's important to clarify a little more miseducation.

The true meaning of the word "heaven" simply put means "skies." The Hebrew word used in Genesis 1 was *shamayim* and is plural meaning "heights or elevations" (Genesis 1:1; 2:1), which can also mean higher dimensions (realms, planes) of existence.

Without going through a whole history of the word *heaven,* somewhere through the centuries and translations it took on another meaning such as "the abode of God." And when we consider what we have already discussed regarding the many beings visiting Earth who were called gods throughout the ages, it makes sense that those witnessing these events would look to the sky and call it the abode of God.

God or Source is also described as the Infinite Intelligence, The One Infinite Creator, and All That Is. All of these names refer to the One from which everything (visible and invisible) emanates. It as Itself (the One Unity) is not physically visible to the human eye (as we comprehend it) where It would come out of the sky and stand before you, saying something like, "Follow this rule or do this because I am God."

Then who is the "God" we read about in the Bible? Who gave Moses the 10 Commandments? Who guided the people through the desert?

When carefully reading just these two events we see that "The Lord" appeared from within dense clouds, on the tops of mountains, and often with intense amounts of fire. Exodus 13:21-22 reads, "And the Lord went before them by day in a pillar of cloud to lead them along the way, and by night in a pillar of fire to give them light, that they might travel by day and by night. The pillar of cloud by day and the pillar of fire by night did not depart from before the people."

Exodus 19:16-18 reads, "On the morning of the third day thunder and lightning, with a thick cloud over the mountain, and a very loud trumpet blast. Everyone in the camp trembled. Then Moses led the people out of the camp to meet with God, and they stood at the foot of the mountain. Mount Sinai was covered with smoke because the Lord descended on it in fire. The smoke billowed up from it like smoke from a furnace, and the whole mountain trembled violently."

When we read these passages and others like them while sitting in Sunday School or in a church service, we are taught about it through the lens of religion. An image of a singular God has already been given to us since childhood, and described as holy, powerful, mysterious, and miraculous. However, today we understand technology and space flight something the people of that time did not.

We can easily look up into the sky and identify an airplane, helicopter, B52, or rocket, etc. We can pull up a video online and hear the loud thunderous sound of the space shuttle. We can see the huge billow of fire and smoke that spew out from a rocket. If we have ever been close to one of these while they are ascending or descending, we know what it is like to see and feel the heat of the flames, smell the smoke, and be moved by the rumbling ground shaking beneath our feet.

It is not strange or miraculous, but it is incredibly awesome to see the power of this kind of technology in action. Now, imagine witnessing a highly advanced craft, one that appears to come from a civilization far beyond ours, perhaps even hundreds of years ahead in the future.

When removing the filter of religion, we see that the scene described in Exodus sounds much like an event like this. A space craft landing on top of Mount Sinai shaking it violently with fire and smoke like a furnace, and Moses is communicating with the advanced being(s) inside. As discussed already, Ezekial, Enoch, other prophets, and Biblical characters described experiencing similar events.

Based on interpretations of the ancient Sumerian tablets and other common scholarly and esoteric texts we find numerous writings about an advanced society of beings who were called *The Anunnaki*. This name translates to "those who came from the heavens."

Detailed accounts of these beings appear throughout the Sumerian tablets, again, these texts are among the oldest written records known to humanity. The writings describe these beings as powerful deities who descended from the sky and played a central role in the shaping of our civilization, agriculture, and our understanding of the cosmos.

These beings are said to be the *gods* we read about in Genesis, known as the Elohim, which was translated into the singular God in the Bible. **These are the creator gods who's patterns, personalities, actions, and rules have been attributed to God or Source**.

The Anunnaki, as mentioned in ancient texts, were not always described with consistent physical features, but the iconography gives us intriguing clues. They are often portrayed as taller and more imposing than humans, with some interpretations suggesting they were giant-like beings. Typically, they appeared in human form, adorned with elaborate beards, muscular physiques, and regal or divine garments.

According to Sitchin's translation of the Cuneiform Tablets, the Anunnaki originated from a planet called Nibiru said to exist beyond Pluto. He described them as approximately 8 to 10 feet tall, with copper-toned skin and genetic advancements that granted them abilities we would consider superhuman.

Many ancient depictions show them with wings, which may symbolize their "heavenly" origin or their ability to move between realms. However, in Mesopotamian art, wings often serve as the symbolic representation of flight.

Recovered artifacts, carvings, and statues depict some of them as hybrid beings, with eagle heads, lion bodies, or serpentine features. These motifs appear in other ancient texts as well. In the Bible, we see similar imagery: the serpent in the Garden of Eden, the winged, multi-faced beings in Ezekiel's encounter, and Goliath, whose enormous size and strength terrified even seasoned warriors.

According to many of these ancient texts, such as The Enuma Elish, the Anunnaki were involved in the evolution of humanity, genetically fashioning homo sapiens initially to serve as their laborers or slaves (their manipulation of the

Homo Erectus DNA, is what is described as the *missing link* in Darwin's Theory of Evolution). The Anunnaki lived among us and traveled back and forth from Earth. We had regular access to them, knowing they were our creators, hence the people called them lord and god.

It is noted in these texts that these beings were also master geneticist and created all types of beings as they were attempting to fashion our species of homo sapiens.

When they came about creating a suitable specimen of individuals (who the Bible calls *Adam and Eve*). The couple was kept in an enclosed garden where the "gods" could regularly monitor them. Genesis 3:8 "Then the man and his wife heard the sound of the Lord God **as he was walking in the garden** in the cool of the day...." This scripture describes God as a physical being walking in the garden, when we know that Source is nonphysical/invisible. (see John 1:18, Colossians 1:15, 1 Timothy 1:17).

These humans initially did not have the awareness of procreation, however once this knowledge was revealed it changed the trajectory of mankind's future. Additionally, they were not the only 2 people in existence, hence we see in Genesis 4 that when Cain was expelled from the garden, he was marked so that no one who found him would kill him.

Some metaphysical texts note that there were several species already evolving on the planet, as well as all of the others created through genetic engineering by the Anunnaki, which also included splicing animal and human DNA.

167

Sidebar: *According to the translation of the tablets by Sitchin*

Genetic engineers*: The Anunnaki created modern humans by splicing their own DNA with that of ancient hominids, essentially making them proto-humans for labor purposes.*

Biblical Adam and Eve*: They were the first successful hybrid beings and were monitored in a controlled environment, consistent with the "garden" motif in the Genesis narrative.*

Limited initial knowledge*: Sitchin suggests these hybrids were initially sterile, akin to mules, until the "knowledge of procreation" was introduced by the Anunnaki deity Enki (who parallels the serpent figure) modifying the human's reproductive capacity.*[55]

Most traditional scholars interpret the Anunnaki as mythological archetypes representing natural forces or royal lineage. However, there are numerous alternative spiritual traditions that view them as ancient extraterrestrial or interdimensional beings whose legacy is encoded in our DNA, who are identified in the Bible as *The Watchers* and *The Sons of God*.[56]

Modern geneticists report that up to 98% of human DNA is considered non-coding, often referred to as "junk DNA." It's puzzling to me that any part of our genetic blueprint would be dismissed or referred to as *junk*, especially when scientists admit they don't yet understand how to interpret it. However, it is extremely likely that some of these professionals *have* uncovered our origins but are not at liberty to disclose this information to the public.

---

[55] Sitchin. The Complete Earth Chronicles. (2014).
[56] Winter. *The Complete Book of Enoch: Standard English Version.* (2015).

Comparative Summary

In metaphysical and alternative historical circles, the question of where humans come from is a powerful one. So I'd like to summarize the parallels of Sitchin's translation of the Sumerian tablets with the information gleaned from the Ra Material and the Cayce Readings.

According to Sitchin's interpretation there were already hominids like *Homo erectus* present on Earth when extraterrestrial beings called the Anunnaki arrived from the planet Nibiru around 450,000 years ago. These visitors came seeking gold (which is a highly useful material for their planetary atmosphere) but instead of mining it themselves, they genetically modified early humans to create a new species: *Homo sapiens.*

Sitchin's narrative suggests that the Anunnaki spliced their own DNA with that of the Earth's primitive hominids, producing a labor force called the "Lulu Amelu," or *"mixed worker."* These beings would later become the ancestors of modern humans. In this account, humanity's origin is not merely evolutionary or divine, but engineered, bridging the gap between science, myth, and spiritual purpose.

The Ra Material. Sitchin's interpretation aligns in many ways with teachings from The Ra Material, which frames humans as spiritual beings evolving through densities, who at times in our history have been influenced and guided by extraterrestrial civilizations. Sitchin's interpretation is based on an ancient human civilization written records therefore gives us a more materialist story. While the Ra Material focuses less on physical human forms and material evolution, seeing this as less important than our soul's evolutionary path, of which this human experience is just a small part.

Edgar Cayce's readings offer yet another perspective, suggesting that souls incarnated into physical matter and became trapped in the material world through misuse of spiritual law. He implied that beings in ancient civilizations like Atlantis experimented with mixing animal and human genetics, echoing the hybrid creation themes of Sitchin's Anunnaki.

Each of these models (whether ancient astronaut or metaphysical) suggests that humanity is far more complex and cosmic in origin than what we have been taught. Whether we were engineered, seeded, or descended from spirit, the consistent thread is this: we are not merely of the Earth, but of the stars, and perhaps something even greater.

Divine Communication and ET Intervention

Let's take a moment to clearly distinguish between the One God of all creation, also called Source, All That Is, or The One Infinite Creator—and the Elohim, who appear across ancient traditions under names such as The Watchers, Sons of God, Anunnaki, Extraterrestrials, or simply the "gods."

These so-called gods are not the One God or Source of all creation, but rather they are advanced beings—created like us, yet older and more evolved in consciousness and technology. Despite their power, they too are beings who originated from the same Source we all share (GOD).

Each of us holds an unbreakable inner connection to that Source. This Divine Intelligence is the essence of everything—you, me, the universe—All That Is. Though nonphysical and beyond ordinary sight, Source expresses Itself through all dimensions of existence, including the physical. As Scripture affirms:

- "By faith we understand that the universe was formed at God's command, so that **what is seen was not made out of what was visible** (Hebrews 11:3)."
- "The Son is the image of **the invisible God** (Colossians 1:15)."
- "**You are all sons** of God through faith in Christ Jesus (Galatians 3:26).

("faith" means belief, not worship. This teacher emphasized that the Kingdom of God is within you.)

Despite religious claims that divine visitations have ceased, communication from Source has never stopped. The One Creator continues to express Itself through Its creation, and the beings (or gods) referenced in sacred and mythological texts still engage with humanity.

Today, this connection may manifest through visions, inspirations, channeling, and even globally witnessed UFO phenomena. Many of which are experienced by several people at a time and well-documented. For example you can look up:

- The Battle over Los Angeles (1942).
- The Phoenix Lights (1997).
- The Floating City over China (2015).
- The Travis Walton Abduction (1975).

Such extraordinary events suggest that both divine presence and extraterrestrial contact continue, waiting for those with eyes to see and hearts open to perceive.

Across the globe reputable archaeologists and geologists have uncovered physical evidence pointing to ancient visitations, evidence that is often explained to the public in ways that defy logic. Megalithic sites like Stonehenge, Machu Picchu, and numerous pyramids have been studied by modern engineers who assert that even with today's most advanced technological machinery, replicating these colossal structures would be impossible.

These experts maintain that, even without fully understanding the methods used, it is clear these structures could not have been built by primitive people using only basic hand tools. While some may attribute their construction to divine intervention or "God," closer examination reveals clear indications of advanced technology at work and physical evidence of materials made up of elements not found on Earth.

Additionally, governments around the world have recovered wreckage from various sites, often documented but hidden from the public, with details revealed by insiders. Many of these insiders are long standing officers of organizations such as the CIA, FBI, and NASA. These include military officials, pilots, and astronauts who have reported and documented phenomenal sitings and experiences.[57]

Dare I mention the millions of people from around the globe reporting abductions annually. Many are doctors, lawyers, teachers, and other sound minded upstanding individuals. When their accounts make it to the mainstream public, they are debunked and explained away as a hoax. However, many go on to write and publish their own books, create documentaries, or become speakers and teachers.

Author Whitley Strieber wrote about his personal abduction experience in his bestselling book, *Communion* (1988). Author and teacher Kaia Ra also discusses her experience meeting a divine presence after spending her childhood as a victim of sex trafficking in her book, *The Sophia Code* (2016). Trauma Surgeon turned disclosure advocate Dr. Steven Greer

---

[57] *Unacknowledged*: An Exposé of the World's Greatest Secret. (2017).

has produced several documentaries relating to human ET contact after personally witnessing unexplained phenomena himself.

We are all waking up and seeing for ourselves that many of these accounts are not fake but real. If you truly understand the Bible, and read it without theological interpretations, it is arguably a main source of written accounts of ET contact evidence. We are not alone in the universe, according to retired NASA Scientist Dr. Richard Hoover, "It would actually be more miraculous if we were." [58]

---

[58] *Ancient Aliens*, season 18, episode 14. (2022).

SOPHIA C. RUSSELL

19 The Trinity of Reality

One God and Father of all, who is above all, and through all, and in all." —Ephesians 4:6

The One God, who I refer to as Source, again, is everything. there is nothing that it is not. This Divine Source originated as the first dimension which according to De Stefano is called Unity, this is where Source pondered what it could become, which opened the door to a second dimension.

According to De Stefano this thought of God produced a split creating positive and negative, and he calls the second dimension, Duality. Bear in mind that I am explaining these happenings in a linear manner for our understanding. From our current human perspective it boggles the mind to conceive events otherwise.

These positive and negative forces continued to split over and over again sort of like cells and repetitively multiply themselves. The continuous movement of positive and negative then created a space between them, neutrality (balance) which created the third dimension, Trinity. De Stefano explains that in the first two dimensions there is no time or experience, only thought. For Source to experience Its thoughts, the third dimension was created.

The continuous splitting produced innumerable positive and negative forces with each splitting moving outward further and further away from Source, until the point between them (neutrality) began pushing them back toward Source. This push creates waves, and these waves are the concepts we call time and space.

175

The waves coalesce into a spiral which then produces the powerful energy we call light and vibration which we call sound. The waves are constantly in motion, moving around ranging from very low and very high, each creating a different vibration (sound or frequency). When all the energy and sounds together move to the core of neutrality, the second dimension (positive and negative, duality) creates form, or matter. The matter makes up the shapes of the universe, it is the way Consciousness moves. These are the states in which the One Mind can experience everything it imagines. You are God experiencing Itself, and so is everyone around you. We are all unique reflections of One Light.

De Stefano explains that the third dimension includes sound (vibration), light (energy), and matter (form). These three are the Trinity which make up reality as we know it and have nothing to do with what is popularly depicted in some religions as the father, the son, and the spirit, or the father, the mother, and the son. These were likely metaphors for human understanding during a time in our history when science and physics were less understood, and life events were typically viewed through a more philosophical or religious lens.

These three (vibration, energy, and form) are not separate from one another but form a tetrahedron. This is what we call *sacred geometry* which is the process by which Consciousness experiences the cosmic plan through form. Everything that is produced by the original Source (God) has the Consciousness of Source within it, giving it the power to create like Itself, through thought. [59]

Each dimension thereafter, the fourth, fifth and so on are designed as an extension of the prior, and all are

---

[59] De Stefano. *Initiation.* Season 1, episodes 1, 2, and 5. (2019).

interconnected forming what is called the flower of life. This flower, though typically invisible to the human eye, is in every physical form in existence. Often used as a symbol of creation and the birth of the universe, the form of the flower represents the process of creation unfolding from a single point of origin, expanding outward to form the complexity of the cosmos. Individuated consciousnesses existing on some levels such as our current one need a physical body while others do not, however, on some of these levels a body can be materialized if needed.

Dimension or Density, what's the Difference?

"Density" and "dimension" are terms commonly used in various fields, including mathematics, physics, statistics, and even social sciences and each has their own way of defining and understanding the concepts. It is common for some to use the two interchangeably though this would be an error. For the sake of this text, I am discussing the metaphysical use of these terms.

According to The Ra Material, dimensions refer to different planes or levels of existence. Everything is ultimately energy, and each dimension represents a unique vibrational frequency of that realm of energy. Dimensions can also be understood as multiple layers of reality that exist simultaneously, with higher dimensions representing higher states of consciousness or awareness.

This is not a hierarchy in the way we might be tempted to understand it. In this context *higher* does not mean the beings in these planes are better than or have lordship over you and me. It also does not mean that they are more moral or *angelic*, as we might perceive them. In this context, both positive and negative beings may evolve and progress through these

177

dimensions as they expand their awareness, power, and connection with The One Consciousness (God).

Densities, on the other hand, refer to the levels of spiritual evolution or development of the beings within each dimension. Each density represents a stage of spiritual growth and awareness. Ra noted that there are varying densities within each dimension, each corresponding to a specific level of consciousness and spiritual advancement. Beings progress through these densities as they evolve spiritually, with each density representing a deeper understanding of universal principles and a closer alignment with the Divine Source.

In summary, dimensions refer to different planes of existence or levels of reality, while densities represent the stages of spiritual evolution held by the beings within each dimension. The concept of dimensions and densities provides a framework for understanding the nature of reality and the spiritual journey of beings within it.

This understanding is essential to space travel and is partly why our mainstream scientific model remains limited; it continues to dismiss these universal principles. However, numerous advanced societies throughout the universe have been reaching out to help us understand them throughout time. There are also numerous physicists, theorists, and scientists working in our government and at our universities who make breakthroughs that go largely ignored, and as a result our societal advancement is stalled.

In efforts to keep this text at an intermediate level, I think this is enough about the fabric of reality for now.

20 Reclaiming Divinity Beyond the Church

"Reports that say that something hasn't happened are always interesting to me, because as we know, there are known knowns; there are things we know we know. We also know there are known unknowns; that is to say, we know there are some things we do not know. But there are also unknown un-knowns — the things we don't know we don't know."
—Donald Rumsfeld, 2002

After nearly two decades as a practicing Christian, I still found myself grappling with fundamental questions, like where I was before being born. Despite my sincere efforts to live a "saved" life and secure my place in "heaven," at the time I could never quite grasp what or where heaven truly was.

I had faith, defined in Hebrews 11:1 as *confidence in what we hope for and assurance about what we do not see.* But like any sincere student exploring a subject deeply meaningful to them, I wanted to know more. Everything I was capable of knowing.

In school, I learned that this type of inquiry falls within the fields of research and science. In these fields, the investigator begins with a question and follows the trail of evidence, keeping their minds open enough to explore every possible explanation. It's through this open and curious approach that some of the world's greatest discoveries are made.

In most major religions, however, we are encouraged to follow along with only what is traditionally accepted and when doing so our minds close, or we simply miss a vast world of viable probabilities. Especially when that information does not coincide with the accepted or "canonized" doctrine.

179

As I sought to know more, I realized that the God in me, was guiding me to knowledge that did not necessarily align with traditional Christian understanding, and as I shared earlier, this scared me at first. But as I learned to embrace a more unconditional view of world history, the nature of the universe, and the diversity of life within it, I felt more and more peace. "For God has not given us a spirit of fear, but of power and of love and of a sound mind (2 Timothy 1:7)."

This understanding coincides with the limitless Source we call God, rather than the finite view we are traditionally taught in our churches which guides us to believe that there is only one species of human, living on only one planet, and we are given only one life to live. The Infinite Creator, however, is not bound by this human ideology and continues to create endlessly anyway.

Sidebar: Why I Say, "The Man We Call Jesus" From Yeshua to Jesus — How the Name Changed.

Many are surprised to learn that the name "Jesus" is not the true name of this historical teacher, nor was it what he would have been called during his lifetime. Born into a Jewish family in first-century Judea, he would have spoken Aramaic, and scholars say that his name would almost certainly have been Yeshua, a common Hebrew/Aramaic name during his time meaning "Yahweh is salvation."

However, there is no birth record that states this teachers name directly, and the conclusion of "Yeshua" is based on linguistic, cultural, and historical indications. Thus scholars widely agree that Yeshua was (most likely) the name he was known by in daily life. The form "Jesus" is the result of a long process of translation and transliteration as his story was carried across centuries, languages, and cultures.

•Hebrew/Aramaic to Greek:

The New Testament was written in Greek, which lacks a "sh" sound. So Yeshua became Iēsous (pronounced i-sis) to fit Greek phonetics and grammar.

•Greek to Latin:

As Christianity spread through the Roman Empire, Iēsous was transliterated into Iesus (pronounced yay-sus) in Latin, the language of the early church.

•Latin to English:

The letter "J" didn't exist in English until the 15th century. As it developed, "Iesus" evolved into Jesus, the form used in the 1611 King James Bible and in modern English today.

No single individual changed this teachers name; rather, it was derived from biblical scholars and evolved gradually over centuries through the process of translation and cultural adaptation. In truth, no one actually knows or has any record of this teachers true name, but we know for sure that it was not Jesus.

Now I ask you, my reader, how can you worship in his name and pray to God through his name, when there is no record of one?

We read in Matthew 7:22–23, "Many will say to me on that day, 'Lord, Lord, did we not prophesy in your name, and in your name drive out demons, and in your name perform many miracles?' Then I will tell them plainly, 'I never knew you. Away from me, you evildoers!'"

This powerful statement suggests something deeper: not only have Christians historically been using another name, but perhaps more importantly, this teacher was not asking to be worshipped, nor was he seeking reverence of his name, but instead he was *showing* us a way of life. His dismissal of their statement in this passage, in my view, reveals a profound message: those who focus on invoking his name have missed the point entirely.

The man we call Jesus and The Christ Consciousness

When people ask me today if I am Christian, I typically ask, "What is a Christian?" They say something like, "A follower of Christ." Though I know they are referring to the man we call Jesus, we can see now that the question itself is flawed, Christ is not a man but is an individuated consciousness (among many) who came out of Source.

This consciousness lived numerous lives eons ago in our time and was the first to make its way back to Source, as we all are on a path of doing. From its experienced, and highly evolved divine state, the Christ Consciousness throughout the ages has manifested itself into form to remind others of the way to accomplish what it already had. Among manifesting as various spiritual teachers throughout Earth's history, one of those was the teacher (likely) named Yeshua.

I do not need to *follow* Christ, for we all are living perspectives of the One Consciousness able to access the Christ consciousness within ourselves. "And I will ask the Father, and he will give you another advocate to help you and be with you forever (John 14:16)."

Just as corporations design marketing strategies to boost profits, societal and religious leaders have carefully crafted the image of Jesus as THE Christ, a calculated act of spiritual branding rooted in two significant mistranslations:

1. The name of the teacher.

2. How The Christ has been defined.

Sadly, For generations this branding has shaped how we perceive salvation and spiritual authority.

In modern life, we regularly use brand names in place of actual products because we've been trained to associate names with meaning and necessity. In a similar way, the image of Jesus has been presented as a spiritual product, a singular mediator between humanity and Source, a necessary product for salvation. And much like corporate advertising, this conditioning often works beneath our awareness, influencing us deeply without our conscious realization.

Take for example, how we use brand names in everyday language: we might ask a coworker to "Xerox" a document, even if the machine is an HP or Brother. Or we refer to all disposable diapers as "Pampers," or sanitary products as "Kotex," or ask for a "Kleenex" instead of tissue, regardless of the actual brand.

These companies executed brilliant marketing strategies that made their names synonymous with the products themselves. Xerox, though once the dominant player in the copier market, is now just one of many brands, but their name still stands in for the entire concept of photocopying. In much the same way, we've also been programmed to refer to one man as *THE* Christ, as if the title belongs exclusively to his personality.

Traditionally, we're taught very little about who the man called Jesus truly was. Most of what we think we know comes solely from the Bible, yet large portions of his life are noticeably absent from it. In addition to his birth name, his teenage years, his daily practices, his diet, even his time spent training in Egypt are left unaddressed. While numerous historical and spiritual accounts explore these missing pieces, much of that information has been kept from the Christian.

In his writings, Seth explains that the figure of Jesus, as traditionally understood, was actually a composite of three separate individuals, each playing a different role in the formation of the Christian narrative. These three figures, in relation to religious history and the development of Christianity is discussed in chapter 21 of *Seth Speaks* (1972). In this text, the idea that religious writings have a deeper symbolic meaning is explored, and that the historical narrative of who we know as Jesus has been shaped by myth, distortion, and misinterpretation over time.

In the Cayce readings "Christ" is not merely a title for Jesus of Nazareth but is a universal consciousness accessible to all souls. The Christ consciousness represents the highest spiritual awareness, a state of perfect unity with divine will, love, and harmony.

The readings, and other metaphysical texts, describe the man we call Jesus, as a soul who, through multiple lifetimes (or incarnations), prepared himself to embody the fullness of this divine state. His mission was to serve as a way-shower (pronounced with long O), demonstrating how individuals could align with divine principles and cultivate the Christ Consciousness within themselves (Cayce Reading 3054-4).

The mistranslation or misunderstanding of baptism

"Jesus replied, 'Very truly I tell you, no one can see the kingdom of God unless they are born again' (John 3:3)."

"Jesus answered, 'Very truly I tell you, no one can enter the kingdom of God unless they are born of water and the

Spirit. Flesh gives birth to flesh, but the Spirit gives birth to spirit' (John 3:5-6)."

We are taught in Christianity to believe these passages are support for the act of baptism, I argue that they are support for reincarnation. Each time a human is conceived, it is fully immersed in water in its mother's womb. For birth to take place, the spirit joins the body, the water breaks, and a new life is born into the world.

The Cayce readings state that the journey toward Christ consciousness involves growth over many lifetimes, as souls learn vital lessons in love, compassion, and spiritual discipline. As you can probably see by reflecting on the current life you are now living, none of us is able to obtain this level of divinity in just one lifetime, which the Bible describes as a "mist" (James 4:14). This universal path bridges humanity with the divine, guiding each soul's journey towards remembering their own unity with Source through many lives and experiences.

The practice of baptism is highly debated among belief systems, only becoming a Christian tradition in the 1st century AD. But it originated from Jewish purification rituals such as mikvah baths, and those practiced by the Essenes, a mystical Jewish sect active during the lifetime of the man we call Jesus. The Essenes practiced ritual washing as part of their daily spiritual discipline, believing it to symbolize spiritual cleansing and renewal.

"Let it be so now; it is proper for us to do this to fulfill all righteousness (Matthew 3:15)." In my view, it is obvious that the teacher initiated being baptized for a different reason than churches baptize today (to save your soul). If Jesus and John were to partake in this event under the rules of today's churches then Jesus would have been baptizing John, as there

185

is no church or religion that would allow the student to baptize the teacher.

In metaphysical teachings, however, the baptism of the man we call Jesus is understood as more than a traditional religious practice. It marked a spiritual turning point in time for humanity. He was initiating an energetic pathway, one that raised the frequency of the planet and invites every soul to realize the Christ pattern within, ushering in an awakening (or spiritual cleansing and renewal) for all of humanity.

The tradition of baptism has evolved over time, with different practices and interpretations emerging at various points in history. Even within the Christian tradition it was not always interpreted as it is today, a necessary step for salvation. Again, you are never separate from your Source. You can be baptized or not, again it is your energetic frequency that aligns you with your experiences. Not only here on the Earth plane but throughout your entire eternal existence.

Because this teacher (who remembered his divine purpose) came to awaken people from the grip of religious legalism and control, and because he did not suffer from the "spiritual amnesia" that most of us do, his baptism marked a profound turning point for humanity. At that time, similar to today, nearly everyone was still "asleep" to the deeper truth of reality.

If we say we are "saved" through him, that may not be entirely inaccurate—but only if we are truly learning from him and living what he taught: that the divine presence dwells within each of us, and that we too embody the same power he did. Just as we might say someone "saved" us from a car accident or a destructive habit like addiction, we could say that this teacher's enlightened words "saved" us by awakening us to a truth we hadn't recognized before. In that sense, yes, he saved us—but not in the way most churches have taught us to believe.

Known as The Great Commission Matthew 28:19-20 we read, "Therefore go and make disciples of all nations, baptizing them in the name of the Father and of the Son and of the Holy Spirit, and teaching them to obey everything I have commanded you. And surely I am with you always, to the very end of the age."

This passage is also highly debated among theologians and religious scholars, some expressing that translators may have misinterpreted older texts. Several metaphysical and esoteric sources offer alternative interpretations that differ significantly from traditional Christian doctrine. These perspectives usually reinterpret baptism and the role of Jesus not as a command to initiate people into religious institutions, but as an energetic, or consciousness-based process of awakening others to divine truth.

In this view, the Great Commission is not a literal command to perform water baptisms or convert others through doctrine, but as an invitation to awaken individuals to their own inner divinity. Practically speaking, how many individuals undergo baptism, experience change for a while, and then eventually return to living the same—or even worse—than they did before? The reason is a lack of understanding about their own energetic frequency.

Teachers like, Cayce, Neville Goddard, Joseph Murphy, and other sources such as *The Urantia Book* or *A Course in Miracles* view baptism as a spiritual initiation or inner transformation. Rather than promoting religious ritual, the man we call Jesus is seen as urging his followers to help others remember their oneness with Source and live from a higher state of consciousness.

Traditional Christion View	Metaphysical Reframe
Baptism = Water ritual for salvation	Baptism = Inner awakening/shift in consciousness
Command to convert in a Trinitarian formula	Initiation to assist others in remembering their divine origin
Discipleship = Religious adherence, *saving* others	Discipleship = Living as an awakened soul and helping others wake up

Another important factor to consider is that historical and religious figures, including Jesus, are shaped by the cultural and spiritual contexts in which they exist. This means that interpretations of the man we call Jesus' life and teachings will vary widely depending on the beliefs and values of different societies not only throughout the world, but also throughout time.

For example, when I was still part of the TikTok corporate workforce, we'd often have periods of downtime where conversations naturally flowed among employees throughout the day. One afternoon, the topic of religion came up. A coworker shared how disorienting it was for her when she moved from Israel to the United States as a young adult and discovered that the man she had worshipped all her life as Yeshua was being called Jesus. She had never known he was referred to by another name. She recalled thinking, "Well, what else has been changed?"

At the time, I still identified as a Christian, yet I had heard very little about the name Yeshua. Even after she shared that insight, I didn't grasp its significance—nor did I feel compelled to question how or why the name had changed. I was still asleep.

A key factor to remember is that while information may be altered or lost in translation, it is the essential teachings of these spiritual figures that should remain our focus, forgiveness, peace, unity, faith, hope, and love. These are universal truths that transcend any single individual or religious belief system.

Rather than getting caught up in debates about who is right or wrong, saved or lost, I encourage you (my readers) to embrace these virtues and prioritize them over disagreements about the historical accounts surrounding the messenger. In reality we couldn't sort through and straighten out all of the thousands upon thousands of ancient texts even with the most well trained translators and advanced technology if we wanted to.

The Christ consciousness is an empowering and attainable spiritual potential, offering a transformative path for all humanity to realize their divine nature and ultimate destiny, and it is not bound to any one person.

Today when I am asked about being a Christian the response I give might be, "Who did Jesus follow? That is who I follow too."

Still our understanding of "follow" may be a bit off. As one does not necessarily "follow" God, but more so expresses God through being. And each of our individual expressions of God look different from one another. Though there may be similarities, no two expressions (beings) will be the same. So why quarrel and argue over our differences, proving our point or trying to be right? Why not learn from one another instead?

21 As Within, So Without: Thought Power

"Just as a body, though one, has many parts, but all its many parts form one body, so it is with Christ."
—1 Corinthians 12:12

If you have read this far, I take it that at minimum you hold some kind of belief in a higher power. However, even those who hold the views of what could be defined as atheistic, at least understand that there is a cosmic source which continuously holds all things in place. This Source (though it has been given many names throughout the ages) is Consciousness and It is constantly expanding.

Source exists as Itself only as The Original Thought (this is the awareness of Itself or Consciousness) and each time Its thoughts manifest and have experiences, It expands into more and more. We are all Gods thoughts manifested.

Just as your parents thought about you before you were born, imagining what you would be like, look like, and sound like, so it is in the One Mind. Your seemingly individual consciousness was brought into *be*ing as God thought what it would be like to be you. Through this thought, you, or your individuated consciousness, became self-aware, creating what some term your "Over Soul." Out of your over soul, came your soul, which created the blueprint of experiencing life as a human on planet Earth.[60]

When you were Divinely created as consciousness, you then had the freedom to go out from God and experience

---

[60] Darryl Anka. *Bashar: Blueprint for Change: A Message from Our Future.* (1990).

yourself as another aspect of the Source, and as anything you imagine. The soul and consciousness are intricately inter-twined. Consciousness is self-awareness or understanding yourself by seeing *an - * other.

As discussed earlier, once the Divine Source (God) real-ized Itself, It wanted to know what It could become. This thought gave way to creation, non-physical and physical, all probabilities and possibilities. Again, it is only because of our human conditioning that we tend to externalize God. When we have been subconsciously programmed to believe that God is out in heaven, it's challenging to wrap our minds around God as an Intelligent Energetic Source residing within us. But when we come to understand that everything is energy (you and I, and all things) we begin to experience an unblocked connec-tion with our Primary Source and are better able to express our life passions.

In the Seth Material, God or the Universal Consciousness is described as the foundational essence of all that exists, *All That Is*, and individuated consciousness' emerge from the Uni-versal Consciousness. Thus, in terms of origin, our conscious-ness precedes the soul. Yours and my consciousness comes out of the One, and though we perceive ourselves as individu-als, each of us is really one unique aspect of the Primary Con-sciousness (God).

If we were to think of God as a prism, each of us represent one facet of the prism. If I represent the left side of the prism, I am going to have an entirely different view of life, perspec-tive, and experience from my side than those who represent the bottom, top, or another side, and none of our views are wrong. It is just that we are experiencing life from a different perspective, and so our ideas will differ. However, each part is needed to hold the prism together.

As referenced in 1 Corinthians 12:12-27. Our Creator has many parts, and all its parts are necessary. Verse 21: "The eye cannot say to the hand I don't need you, and the head cannot say to the feet, I don't need you." Verse 25: "...so that there should be no division in the body, but that its parts should have equal concern for each other."

Though many different sects of Christians use this passage as support for their particular church community or belief system, it is a guide for the entire cosmos, as everything in existence is the body of God.

When we use this scripture to define only our particular church or only *our part* of the body, we are doing exactly what this passage is teaching us *not* to do. Additionally, when we take the stand that *our* path or way *is the only path* to salvation and another's way is wrong, it is the same as the eye telling the hand it doesn't need it. If I am traveling from the south towards the north, my path will be very different from those traveling from west to north. Same destination different route.

Differences should draw us closer to one another, being open and eager to understand each other's viewpoint, learning from one another, and honoring everyone's perspective as a valid part of the One. It doesn't mean that you have to agree or join in with what works for someone else, it just means that you are honoring another's perspective as a useful and valuable part of God's body. You do not need to change from being an eye to becoming a foot. Or, you can remain a foot and still respect the validity of the eye and the other parts, learning to work together as one cohesive unit.

This understanding promotes empathy and brings harmony, which binds all differences without changing them. Like the harmonic voices of a choir. The soprano does not try to correct the alto, convincing them to sing in her key.

193

Together, they rehearse and learn how to harmonize their voices, not change them.

Sidebar: Iron Sharpens Iron

I once heard an entertainer say that working alongside someone more seasoned in their craft pushes them to elevate their own performance. At the same time, the expert is often inspired and invigorated by the raw talent and fresh perspective of the apprentice. It's a mutual exchange—growth through contrast, refinement through relationship.

The same is true in our spiritual paths. No matter where we are on the journey, we each have something to learn and something to offer. When we come together with open hearts and respect, our differences become strengths, and we all rise.

However, it has been mankind's pattern throughout the ages, to control one another through divisive ideas of right and wrong, leading to all sorts of practices which cause disharmony amongst the masses. This disharmony is against our nature. It can block us from knowing our connection with the Source and interrupts the free flow of energy throughout our bodies. This not only shortens our life span, but it also causes chaos and disorder, as we can look around the world and see. We are all singing a song, and many parts are grossly off key and out of tune.

This disharmony may also be present in your interpersonal relationships. Where you are consistently fighting and arguing with the people whom you "love" the most. I see it in couples regularly; one tries to discuss a problem they have with the other, and the other is immediately offended, expressing their disagreement through anger, which is then met with equal or even heightened force by the other. Both are trying to be heard without listening. Individually, each of them has been entertaining negative mental chatter in their minds constantly about their partner. They haven't even noticed all of the arguing already going on in their minds long before they spoke it out loud. Though it has been made a pun, dare I say, "Can we all just get along?"

It is imperative to examine yourself first, your own thoughts, emotions, and behaviors and you will begin to uncover unconscious (programmed) beliefs which produce all sorts of mental difficulty. Eventually, this impacts your mental health, leading to blocks and impediments in your life goals and in your physical body, in time resulting in discomfort and *dis-ease*. Most *so called* "incurable" diseases are not "caught" through contact, they develop overtime through continued neglect of self-reflection and self-awareness. Through the disconnection of our own mind, body, and spirit. Notice the word is *dis* ease, meaning *not at ease*. Only I have the power to put myself back at ease.

Scriptures such as Matthew 7:1-5 teach us to work on ourselves before calling someone else out on their flaws. Notice that the scripture directs us to "remove the plank from your own eye, and then you will see clearly to remove the speck from your brother's eye."

The eyes were used in the metaphor indicating blindness to one's own faults, disabling them from seeing clearly enough to assist another. Even if you recognize your imperfections as part of being human, the deeper question remains: Are you actively doing the inner work to grow and evolve? Or are you still giving knee jerk reactions to challenges and justifying your behavior by blaming the situation, circumstance, or person involved? Saying things like, "I got so angry because *you* did this or that." Not realizing you could have chosen to respond differently, regardless of the other's behavior. As Plato wisely said, "The unexamined life is not worth living for the human."

Notice also that a plank is significantly larger and far more intrusive than a spec. In my view this means that working on myself is much more important and a priority over "assisting" another.

John 8:7-11 "When they kept on questioning him, he straightened up and said to them, 'Let any one of you who is without sin be the first to throw a stone at her.' Again, he stooped down and wrote on the ground. At this, those who heard began to go away one at a time, the older ones first, until only Jesus was left, with the woman still standing there. Jesus straightened up and asked her, 'Woman, where are they? Has no one condemned you?' 'No one, sir,' she said. 'Then neither do I condemn you.' Jesus declared. 'Go now and leave your life of sin.'

In this passage the teacher, without condemnation, calls everyone involved, the accuser and the accused, to examine themselves.

Medical research has shown that a common thread linking people suffering from cancer, arthritis, heart disease, digestive issues, diabetes, poor mental health, and general pain, is years of negative thoughts and perception which were typically brought on by past unresolved trauma.[61] [62] Though you may have experienced some awful things in your life, they do not have to continue to control you all throughout your journey, and only *you* have the power to change it. "No situation or event has meaning; we give it meaning and then respond to that meaning." –Bashar as channeled by Daryl Anka.

---

[61] Robert H Pietrzak, et al. (2012).
[62] Karen A Schlauch, et al. (2022).

Sidebar: Cohesion of The Heart and Mind

"As a man thinketh, in his heart so is he (Proverbs 23:7)." I must confess, I moved the comma in this passage as it was originally placed after the word "heart." Through deeper study, however, I realized something more significant: we don't actually think with the heart, we feel with it. And those feelings stem from our thoughts, which then influence our behavior. As we think we are, we feel we are, and so we behave.

Each thought we entertain gives rise to a feeling in the heart, and those feelings shape our behavior. When the heart and mind are not aligned, the heart can mislead us, resulting in choices that later feel out of sync with who we truly are. Cultivating coherence between heart and mind is so important before taking action, especially when something feels off.

One clear sign of this misalignment is when you find yourself giving someone "the benefit of the doubt" while ignoring your own inner knowing. That tension is your signal, your guidance system nudging you toward alignment. Jeremiah 17:9 "The heart is deceitful above all things and beyond cure. Who can understand it?" Proverbs 4:23 "Above all else, guard your heart, for everything you do flows from it."

Try this, the next time a person or event has your attention focused in a negative or unwanted direction, before discussing it with anyone, stop for a moment and examine your thoughts and the emotion they produce in you. Then see if it is possible to think about the issue differently (more positively) and pay attention as your emotion changes.

For example, let's say you come out of the store, you see at a distance there seems to be a big dent in your car door. An immediate thought might be, "Damn! Some bleep bleep hit my door." The feelings that follow that thought may be irritability or frustration. Realizing what's done is done, you get in the car and continue to ponder the matter in your head. Your thoughts will either amp you up or calm you down.

You might think, *"What a jerk, they could have left a note. I hope somebody hits their car. It will probably be hundreds of dollars to fix. I barely have enough money as it is…"* The thoughts go on and on.

As you think this way stress and tension grow stronger. Your emotions may change from irritation to full blown anger. You get home and snap at a loved one, then bark at them telling them what happened. Subsequently, they join you in your anger, adding more worry to the matter. Now the event has taken on a negative momentum that is getting stronger. Next you hear that insurance won't cover it and so on.

Now imagine the same scenario, you approach the vehicle see the dent, and think the same thing, "Damn! Some bleep bleep hit my door." However, this time you pause and notice the irritability. You decide *"I don't want this feeling."* You catch it and change the course of your thinking on purpose. *"Well, it could have been worse. The person was probably afraid, maybe they didn't have insurance or enough money, so they fled. Hopefully, my insurance will cover it, but if not, I'll figure it out."*

You will feel the difference in your body when deescalating instead of amplifying the negative. It is also important to be mindful of discussing the experience with others. If it is not necessary to repeat it then don't. As you grapple with creating a positive outcome and repeat it to someone who is not in tune with their own thought power, you may unintentionally align with a negative outcome. Be mindful of where you focus your attention, as the dominant energy will be amplified. This technique takes practice, and it is important to be honest with yourself about where your emotions are. It's good to identify, "I'm irritated." Acknowledge whatever the emotion is, it needs it, but it does not have to be expressed with full vented aggression.

Our tendency is to resist or push against negativity when this is not necessary. Negativity has its own purpose of helping us to move forward (remember **everything** is God). So though is feels uncomfortable, it is ok to accept that negativity is present and then shift your focus to your preferred outcome.

The idea is to regulate emotion, so that you do not end up amplifying or suppressing it. Overtime suppressed emotions will find another way of expression often through physical pain or illness. Your goal is the sweet spot, the quiet space between suppression and amplification, *balance*. Learning the difference between reacting and responding is key in finding this balance.

It seems like a simple thing. But MOST people are thinking thousands of thoughts daily without knowing that they are creative and shaping the course of their own life experience. We believe our thoughts are *just* thoughts and as long as they are in our own minds they don't matter and have no impact. Thought is your God power. Your thoughts matter and are literally creating your reality.

Philippians 4:8 "Finally, brothers and sisters, whatever is true, whatever is noble, whatever is right, whatever is pure, whatever is lovely, whatever is admirable, if anything is excellent or praiseworthy, **think** about such things."

Romans 12:2 "Do not conform to the pattern of this world but be transformed by the renewing of your mind. Then you will be able to test and approve what God's will is…"

Ephesians 4:23 "...to be made new in the attitude of your minds..."

Colossians 3:2 "Set your minds on things above, not on earthly things."

These passages invite us to go deeper than surface-level behavior and examine the true source of our experience, our thoughts. Thoughts are the seeds; emotions are the water; behavior is the fruit. The real work lies in transforming our inner dialogue (mental chatter) and aligning it with higher consciousness. Yet many churches, in my experience, prioritize behavior correction over thought renewal, which can feel like tending to the leaves on a tree while ignoring the roots.

This often leads to inner conflict and duality, struggling to maintain an appearance of righteousness while feeling lost inside. We strive to *act* holy while, inwardly we feel like we are fake, stuck, or unworthy. Subsequently, we may attempt to cope with the emotional pain by becoming addicted to behaviors that do not benefit us. Real change begins with learning to observe, guide, and redirect our thoughts, to consciously renew the mind and to bring the heart and mind into coherence with divine truth. In scripture, we are urged to "take every thought captive" (2 Corinthians 10:5).

When we learn to examine and align our thoughts with higher truth, transformation flows naturally from the inside out and often change happens with ease. You will suddenly find that you are no longer interested in certain experiences, people, or conversations that were once exciting to you, and as you realize this, it may be surprising. Some who know you may draw closer while others may grow distant. Though this may feel strange initially, you will acclimate because you are on the path to remembering your true self, God.

22 The Soul's Blueprint

"The trouble is that you consider your soul as a finished static 'thing' that belongs to you but is not you. Your soul is your most intimate powerful inner identity. It is and must be forever changing. It is alive, responsive, and curious. It forms the flesh and the world that you know and is in a state of becoming." —Seth Speaks, 1972

The Seth Material presents a holistic and interconnected view of consciousness and the soul, emphasizing the dynamic and evolving nature of existence and the central role of consciousness in the soul's journey.

Before coming into a human life, the soul is in a nonphysical state and uses consciousness as a means to explore and experience different aspects of reality. While consciousness provides the soul with the necessary tools and perspectives to facilitate its growth and evolution. Think of the soul as the eternal voyager, and consciousness as the vehicle through which it navigates the vast and varied landscapes of existence.

In this state yours and other individuated souls may create groups or "families" as we may better understand them and together plan out the roles and parts we will play in each other's lives here on Earth. From this perspective, we actually do decide who will act as parents and who will act as children. So, the old saying, "Well you don't get to pick your family" is actually not true.

For those who might have difficulty accepting the poor job they feel their parents have done in raising them, or for those parents who are consistently critical of their child's choices, take a moment to close your eyes and ask yourself why you would have chosen the individual to play the role they have played in your life.

For instance, maybe your father left when you were young, or you felt your mother failed you as a parent. Perhaps you are a parent yourself, watching your child make one painful decision after another. In humility, pause and ask yourself: *How has this relationship shaped me? How does it affect my daily life? In what ways have I allowed their behavior to influence my thoughts and emotions? What have I learned, about myself, about others, about relationships and communication? Can I forgive myself and/or the other? Can I release blame?*

As challenging as it is, if you reflect on these questions with honesty, you might discover that this relationship, flawed as it may be, offered you insights and growth you wouldn't have gained otherwise. Your biggest challenges are your most profound teachers.

Sidebar: Earth — Prime Cosmic Real Estate

According to many metaphysical teachings and channeled sources, Earth holds a rare and highly sought-after position within the cosmos. Often described as "prime real estate for soul growth," the planet was intentionally designed as a multidimensional classroom—one rich with emotional depth, energetic potential, and an extraordinary variety of life. Which, I learned through my research, are unique qualities to this planet.

Dolores Cannon's regression clients consistently described Earth as a living library, a place where countless species from across the universe contributed to a vast experiment in consciousness. Similarly, Barbara Marciniak's Pleiadian messages portray Earth as a sacred site of evolution, where souls from many star systems incarnate to grow, experience polarity, and ultimately remember their divine origin.

However, not all influences have been benevolent. As Edgar Cayce's readings suggested, and as echoed by both Cannon and Marciniak, Earth has also experienced interference. As discussed in chapter 18, certain factions of the advanced beings who arrived here in our remote past, recognized the planet's unique energetic signature and the innocence of its early inhabitants, began manipulating the evolutionary path through genetic modification, spiritual suppression, and fear-based control systems.

Despite this deviation, Earth remains a powerful portal for awakening. Beneath the layers of distortion, the original divine design still pulses. Humanity's task now is to reclaim its sovereignty, awaken to the truth of who we are, and realign with the higher purpose Earth was always meant to serve.[63] [64] [65]

We are here to learn, grow, and take a spirit of knowledge back with us.

According to 2 Peter 1:3, we have already been given *everything we need* for life and godliness through divine power. And Ephesians 1:4 affirms that we were *chosen in Him before the foundation of the world.* These scriptures suggest that our existence is not accidental or haphazard, we arrived with purpose, equipped with the tools necessary to navigate this life. From a spiritual perspective, this implies that much was set in place before our birth: inner resources, gifts, and even certain

---

[63] Dolores Cannon. *The Three Waves of Volunteers and the New Earth.* (2011).

[64] Barbara Marciniak. *Bringers of the Dawn: Teachings from the Pleiadians.* (1992).

[65] The Edgar Cayce Readings. Reading 364-1 and 262-39. (A.R.E. Press).

lessons or challenges we agreed to face as part of our soul's evolution.

In this view, incarnation is not a random occurrence, but a deliberate and wise selection made by the soul. Though we forget these decisions upon entering the physical world, they remain imprinted in our deeper consciousness, subtly guiding us back toward alignment with our greater purpose.

In the Seth Material, and in numerous other channeled sources, it is explained that before we enter a human life, we exist as multidimensional, eternal consciousness. As our true self or oversoul, we choose to experience physical reality for the purpose of growth, creativity, and expansion, and this is difficult to do without adding challenges to the plan.

Prior to birth, our soul participates in the planning of each incarnation. Again, it is at this interval that we choose the circumstances, time period, family, and even major life challenges, based on what will offer the most meaningful opportunities for learning and expression.

This decision is not made in isolation; it involves collaboration with other souls, including those with whom we have karmic or developmental ties. This means we may enter into soul agreements, choosing to share certain life experiences with another soul to support each other's growth in a specific way. I am sure many of you can attest to meeting someone new, clicking right away, and feeling deeply that you already knew them. We might sometimes call these soul mates.

However, from a higher perspective we make agreements with who will be our *"enemies"* as well. These are the challenges that offer enormous opportunities for our soul's expansion. So, understand that though it is easy to believe that our life partner is a soul mate, your most difficult relationship might be as well.

Sometimes, if a lifetime ends but the shared plan remains unfulfilled, we may choose to return and try again. This cycle can be repeated until the agreement is honored or until one or both souls decide to release it and move on.

Importantly, each source of channeled material emphasizes that these choices are never forced, they are always guided by free will, purpose, and love. We do not come here to be punished or tested, but to create, evolve, and remember who we truly are, powerful, eternal beings momentarily focused in physical form.

There are often specific themes our souls choose to explore in each lifetime, and again, we design these experiences to support our evolution. We might seek to understand sadness, trauma, joy, or the complexities of relationships. Some souls choose to experience fame, wealth, or poverty, while others explore humility, illness, or loss. To deepen our understanding, we often choose to incarnate from different perspectives, living as male in some lives and female in others. We choose to exist as different cultures, races, and in a variety of social roles. We may mix and match any combination of these, after all we have eternity.

We may decide to live fast and die young in one life and live a long, quiet life in another. Each variation offers a unique lens through which we expand our soul's awareness. From this "other side" we understand human emotions conceptually, but not their full impact. By immersing ourselves in these lived experiences, we grow, evolve, and contribute to the ever-expanding consciousness of the soul, and ultimately to the One Consciousness, God.

205

I've heard one teacher say living a life on Earth is a master's class, so without judging *"how"* you are doing, you should be proud of yourself just for living it out. According to these teachers, the life "blueprint" we create is embedded within us, and we can tune into the guidance anytime.[66]

Before entering into this existence, we knew we would need certain things to support ourselves in the time/space reality we decide to incarnate into (currency, shelter, social support, etc.) and have it all already, in sort of a holding pattern, available to manifest upon request. Spiritual teacher and author Esther Hicks calls this a vortex of creation. This is the truth behind Matthew 7:3, "Ask, and it will be given to you; seek, and you will find; knock, and it will be opened to you."

We understand, even before coming here, that the most challenging aspect of the Earth experience would be the agreement to forget where we came from and who we truly are. Again, this intentional *amnesia* makes the journey feel real and immersive, but also incredibly difficult. To help ourselves along the way, we built certain reminders into our blueprint, little wake-up calls, or breadcrumbs scattered along our path so to speak. These might come as a gentle nudge: such as stumbling upon a video, crossing paths with a teacher or stranger who sparks a meaningful conversation, or being drawn to a particular book (like this one, HELLO!).

If the gentle reminders don't get our attention, the wake-up calls may grow louder, perhaps through a sudden illness, an accident, or a life-altering challenge, anything that shakes us out of the illusion and brings us back to our truth. The fact that you are here, right now, reading this book, is no accident. Your soul orchestrated this very moment as a marker on your

---

[66] Anka. *Bashar: Blueprint for Change: A Message from Our Future.* (1990).

path, a signpost guiding you back to your inner knowing, helping you remember who you are.

"I am a soul having a human experience." My Journey of Remembering

My soul, conscious, alive, and divine. Or God expressing Itself as me, moves through this life as a woman, shaped by the blending of cultures through my earthly parents. Each gift I bear, every flaw I uncover, all of my joys and sorrows alike, are brushstrokes on the canvas of my becoming. Through them, my soul walks its sacred path, ever unfolding, ever returning to the truth of who I Am.

Since reading that first book, *The Esoteric Encyclopedia of Eternal Knowledge* (which I consider a signpost to my personal awakening) I have since been guided to many others. *Bringers of the Dawn,* for example, I found while on Google searching for something completely off topic. This is a collection of teachings from the Pleiadians, who are another group of multidimensional spirit beings from the Pleiades star system. Since 1988, these messages have been channeled through the author Barbara Marciniak, offering profound wisdom for those ready to receive it.[67]

This book discusses the concept of *way-showers* (with a long o) and refers to certain souls who have intentionally incarnated on Earth during times in history of great transition. **We are currently living in such a time.** These way-showers did not choose this time period for their own personal growth only, but more so to help awaken humanity and guide others toward higher consciousness. Way-showers are not here to

---

[67] Marciniak. *Bringers of the Dawn: Teachings from the Pleiadians.* (1992).

"save" or "convert" but to *live as examples* of awakened, free beings who embody love, truth, and multidimensional awareness. Way-showers activate change by transforming themselves first, thereby serving as living blueprints of what is possible for all.

According to the texts, they help anchor light and new frequencies into the planet, inspiring others to reclaim their power, remember their divine origin, and participate consciously in humanity's evolutionary leap. These are not "special" people to be worshipped; they are simply loving souls who want to assist. Perhaps they hadn't intended on incarnating, but decided they possess skills that are useful in assisting others during this time.

These skills might be as simple as being peaceful, helpful, or nurturing. Or maybe they incarnated as an entertainer who could influence many. Or perhaps the mom in the neighborhood who cooks for everyone, or the father in a family where in previous generations no men stuck around, or a teacher, a scientist, or an author. As you can see, there are many.

However, due to the density of our current dimension and the amnesia of the Earth plane, many way-showers temporarily forget their purpose and become entangled in fear, distraction, or societal conditioning. In these cases, they may require reminders, synchronicities, or assistance from other awakened beings to help them remember who they are and why they came.

After reading the text, I was awakened to my true purpose as a way-shower and I could not rest until I wrote this book. It is my hope that not only through this texts, but through my life experiences (both positive and negative) to awaken what the scriptures call the remnants, the elect, these are the way-showers. There are thousands of other way-showers who, like me, have also fallen deep into slumber (or as the Bible would say, they have become of the world) forgetting their purpose of helping others to wake up. Again, this is not separation, converting, or saving, it is simply remembering who we all are.

Some of us incarnated primarily for soul expansion, other's (way-showers) only incarnated to assist with awakening, with the added bonus that there is still growth. Both types have fallen asleep. So, we have had the added layer of communicating with those consciousness who chose not to incarnate and assist from the other side. All are working feverishly together at this crucial time in our history.

As the Earth is also going through her own planetary shift into higher consciousness, it is likely that in the very near future (within the next 10 years, give or take) the shift we will experience here will be catastrophic for those who are still asleep. We read of this warning in Matthew 24 and Mark 13, which also notes that *even the elect could be deceived.*

During your *Soul Walk* here on Earth, you will continuously be presented with challenges that have the tendency to aid in your growth and understanding. Only you know what choices are best for your path, and you learn to choose wisely by connecting with your inner guidance. Wisdom is within you, learn to be silent and listen to her. If at any point you feel guidance is needed, ask for it in prayer. You will be guided to the necessary person, event, or experience which will aid, the same as you were guided to read this book.

When a person, teacher, loved one offers suggestions or advice, be open to it, taking it into prayer and meditation. Ponder how it feels for you. Sometimes you will resonate with it and sometimes you will not. Just remember, it is ok to ask questions for clarity, and it is ok to take the advice or not.

Our Source does not judge your choices in the way we are traditionally taught. We are born knowing that we are visitors here, that we will bump up against difficult conditions and circumstances, that we will make errors and miss the mark, that there is a lot to learn. We know we will transition out of the body; the same way we entered into it.

There is no death, so whatever you experience (rather you view it as fun, easy, challenging, awful, or a huge mistake) the situation can still bring growth and learning if you allow it. However easy or difficult, there is always expansion.

23 Death as a Doorway

"Death is like taking off a tight shoe." —Ram Dass

When we experience what is commonly called "death," our consciousness does not cease to exist, it simply shifts into another state of awareness. In truth, death is not an end but a transformation, a reorganization of our energy into a different form. Perhaps we should not speak of death at all, but of *transition* or *passing on*, for as beings of energy, we do not truly die. Like water turning to steam, we change form, subtle yet continuous. From our human perspective we move from the physical back to nonphysical, from visible to invisible, from seen to unseen.

The moment consciousness leaves the physical body; we enter a phase that reflects our personal energetic frequency. That is our personal beliefs, expectations, and level of spiritual development. Initially, many individuals experience environments that mirror their earthly understanding or core beliefs. Some may perceive a heavenly setting, while others may enter a dreamlike or symbolic realm. That is, if we pass over believing at our core that we will face hell or damnation, we will have this experience. Not because we were *sent* there due to our "sins" but because we are creating it through our thoughts and true beliefs.

This is why it is important to release our loved ones with joy and peace during their passing, rather than clinging to grief, sorrow, or attachment. These lower emotions can create energetic tethers that make it harder for the departing soul to fully transition into their next state of being. By sending them off with love, gratitude, and a sense of celebration for their

211

time here, we support their soul's evolution and allow healing to flow more freely for both them and us. This does not mean you have to suppress sorrow, cry if you need to. I suggest that while doing so, you mindfully guide your thoughts to those of appreciation and thanksgiving for the shared experience.

However, even if an individual does get a little "stuck" eventually, the personality realizes it is no longer bound to the experience and will be aided by guides or loved ones in "snapping out of it" so to speak.

According to the Seth material, these transitional stages help the soul acclimate as it returns to its nonphysical state, where time and space function very differently. In this expanded state, we review our past life, what some call a "life review" or what has been mistakenly viewed as "facing judgement." But this evaluation is not a negative type of judgment, it is a means of gaining clarity and understanding. A period where we gain insight into the impact of our actions, thoughts, and emotional patterns. We evaluate our blueprint, and may ask ourselves certain questions such as, *Did I do what I planned? In what ways have I grown from this life? What did I learn? How has this contributed to my expansion? How did I impact others?* And so on.

For many, this stage of reflection is profoundly difficult, as it includes *feeling* the emotional experience we created for others through our words and actions. Because of this we will be supported by experienced guides, ancestors, or loved ones who passed over before us. Though you may not realize it, it is likely that these beings are with you now as you are living, which helps the passing over to be a smoother transition. Some describe it as sort of feeling just like waking up in the morning.

From a broader, soul-level perspective, each being reflects on its journey, evaluating growth, lessons learned, and areas still unfolding. This reflection helps determine what comes next: whether to reincarnate into another life, explore different dimensions of existence, or serve as a guide for others still on their path.

Crossing over from the human experience does not instantly transform you into an "angel" or an advanced spiritual being. This post-life evaluation is significant as it aids in determining what might be helpful as the soul continues to evolve, gradually returning to Source through cycles of learning and experience. And it's equally important to remember that you retain *free will*. You have the power to choose your next steps, your next realm, and how you wish to continue your soul's unfolding journey. As you tune into your inner world now, your passing over will not be as fearful, and you can make these decisions with clarity, not confusion.

The overarching truth is that consciousness is eternal, creative, and always evolving. Death, then, is not a termination, but a powerful return to a more fluid and expansive form of existence, who you really are.

The Cayce readings explain that after death the soul moves into the spirit world, transitioning through various planes of consciousness that correspond to the planetary spheres (e.g., Mercury, Venus, Mars). These planes are like realms of learning and reflection, where the soul reviews its life, the lessons learned, and how closely it aligned with spiritual ideals such as love, patience, and service. The soul does not face judgment from an external God but engages in self-evaluation, assisted by spiritual guides. Eventually, the soul plans its next incarnation or continues evolving in the non-physical realms.

In the Ra teachings, death is described as the transition of the mind/body/spirit complex from the physical to the metaphysical realms. After physical death, the soul enters a healing and review process in another time/space dimension (what we might call the astral plane). Here, it evaluates its life with the guidance of higher-dimensional beings and prepares for the next step in its spiritual evolution. Depending on the lessons learned and the balance between service to self and service to others, the soul may reincarnate or move forward in its density progression, advancing toward unity with the One Infinite Creator.

Though the Cayce readings were conducted and documented during the early 1900's, decades before The Seth Material, The Ra Material, and other modern metaphysical texts, we can see that the death experience is defined in much the same way. This is not because they stem from any religion, but because they reflect the fundamental truths of Creation itself, the true nature of reality. This truth transcends time and continues to emerge through various teachers (such as the man we call Jesus) across the ages. Still, it is only recognized by those whose hearts and minds are open to hearing it. (See The Parable of the Sower in Matthew 13).

My hope is that you come to realize that you are consciousness, born in the One Mind, God. From this Source emerges individuated consciousness/oversouls, which in turn create many individual souls, each crafting unique blueprints for physical experiences. These experiences, lived through your personality, are designed to gather wisdom in diverse forms of being. At physical *death* (or transition) the wisdom gained becomes spirit, which merges back with the soul and helps guide you on your return to the One Mind. In this way, you contribute to the ever-expanding All That Is, and you have eternity to complete this sacred walk.

As we reach the end of this text, remember that *Soul Walk* is not just a collection of insights, but an invitation, a call to reclaim the sacred knowing already encoded within you. You are not merely a body walking through time; you are a timeless soul walking through dimensions, living, feeling, loving, and re-discovering your divine origin.

Ultimately, there is nothing to fear. The questions you carry, about God, the universe, your purpose, are not signs of doubt, but awakenings of ancient memory. May you now walk forward more consciously, knowing that you are both the seeker and the Source, both the question and the answer. You are not lost, you are becoming. And your soul walk has only just begun.

*"All right, just absorb it in your own way. It doesn't matter how you interpret this information. It's your own journey, your own path. You are your own reflection. You are your own representation of All That Is, and without your unique perspective All That Is, couldn't be, All That Is. So always please remember you are valid, you are valuable, because if you weren't needed, believe me you wouldn't exist because All That Is doesn't make mistakes. So, the fact that you exist is validation enough to prove that All That Is needs your unique perspective, your unique reflection, your unique experience, in order for it to actually be all that **It** can be."—Bashar as channeled by Daryl Anka*

SOPHIA C. RUSSELL

Continue your *Soul's Walk* with the

Soul Walk
Companion Workbook

A sacred space for reflection, integration, and connection.

Inside you'll find:

• Guided prompts and journaling exercises

• Space to process your awakening experiences

• Practical tools for realignment and self-discovery

Available now wherever books are sold.

Learn more at:

www.prosperityhouse.co

SOPHIA C. RUSSELL

Channels & Teachers

Contemporary Channels

Darryl Anka (channels Bashar) https://www.bashar.org/home

Lee Carroll (channels Kryon) https://kryonmasters.com/

Matías De Stefano (channels various beings) https://matiasdestefano.org

Sheila Gillette (channels Theo) https://asktheo.com/

Esther Hicks (channels Abraham) https://www.abraham-hicks.com/

Barbara Marciniak (The Pleiadian Collective) https://www.pleiadians.com/

Jamillah A. Shabazz (channels The Angel) https://seekangelguidance.com/

Tina Spalding (channels Jesus and Ananda) https://channelingjesus.com/

"Interviews with Extra-Dimensionals" is a television series created and hosted by Reuben Langdon, in which he conducts in-depth conversations with various channelers. The show currently spans three seasons with over 60 episodes, and is available for streaming on the Gaia Network. https://www.interviewwithed.org/

Teachers and/or Authors

Queen Afua https://www.queenafua.com/

Michael Bernard Beckwith https://www.michaelbeckwith.com/

Billy Carson https://www.4biddenknowledge.com/

Dr. Joe Dispenza https://drjoedispenza.com/

Neville Goddard (1905 - 1972) https://www.thepowerofawareness.org/

Joel S. Goldsmith (1892 - 1964) https://joelgoldsmithstreaming.com/

Dr. Steven Greer M.D. https://drstevengreer.com/

Dr. J.J. & Dr. Desiree Hurtak https://hurtak.com/

Reverend Ike (1935 - 2009) https://www.revikelegacy.com/

Dr. Joseph Murphy PhD. (1898–1981) https://josephmurphy.wwwhubs.com/

Kaia Ra https://kaiara.com/

Dr. Sebi (1933 - 2016) https://sebisdaughters.com/

Eckhart Tolle https://eckharttolle.com/

Alan Watts (1915 - 1973) https://alanwatts.org/

Stuart Wilde (1946 - 2013) https://www.stuartwilde.com/

References

"*Ancient Aliens on Location: The UFO Investigations.*" Ancient Aliens, season 18, episode 14, History Channel, 29 July 2022. Featuring Dr. Richard Hoover. The HISTORY Channel, 30 May 2025, https://youtu.be/kgGRz6vZHKM?si=dzHepb9uWpgbcY5u.

Anka, Darryl (channeling Bashar). *Bashar: Blueprint for Change – A Message from Our Future*. Edited by Luana Ewing, New Solutions Publishing, 1990.

Bible Gateway. *The Holy Bible*, New International Version, https://www.biblegateway.com/.

Cannon, Dolores. *The Convoluted Universe*: Book One. Ozark Mountain Publishing, 2001.

Cannon, Dolores. *The Three Waves of Volunteers and the New Earth*. Ozark Mountain Publishing, 2011.

Capra, Fritjof. *The Tao of Physics: An Exploration of the Parallels Between Modern Physics and Eastern Mysticism*. 3rd ed., Shambhala Publications, 1991.

Cayce, Edgar. *Edgar Cayce Readings*. Association for Research and Enlightenment, https://edgarcayce.org/edgar-cayce/.

"Cleansing and Renewal: An Early History of Baptism." *GetOrdained.org*, 2020, getordained.org/blog/cleansing-and-renewal-an-early-history-of-baptism.

De Stefano, Matías. *Initiation*. Gaia, season 1, episodes 1, 2, and 5, aired 30 Sept.–14 Oct. 2019. Gaia, https://www.gaia.com/series/initiation.

"Dr. Sebi: Eat to Live (Full Length)." *YouTube*, uploaded by Manifest Media Network and Darius Covington, uploaded 22 Nov. 2013, https://youtu.be/jzVqEfXJHVc?si=J7Sjdh5vjAZQxilH.

"Dr. Sebi talks about his Supreme Court case with Rock Newman." *The Rock Newman Show*, YouTube, uploaded 15 Nov. 2015, https://www.youtube.com/watch?v=y4J8BxbqXOA.

Dunn, Christopher. *The Giza Power Plant: Technologies of Ancient Egypt*. Bear & Company, 1998.

Ehrman, Bart D. *Lost Christianities: The Battles for Scripture and the Faiths We Never Knew.* Oxford University Press, 2003.

Ehrman, Bart D. *Misquoting Jesus: The Story Behind Who Changed the Bible and Why.* HarperOne, 2005.

Ferguson, Everett. *Baptism in the Early Church: History, Theology, and Liturgy in the First Five Centuries.* Eerdmans, 2009.

Hall, Manly P. *The Secret Teachings of All Ages*. Philosophical Research Society, 1928.

Hicks, Esther, and Jerry Hicks. *The Astonishing Power of Emotions: Let Your Feelings Be Your Guide*. Hay House, 2007.

Hicks, Esther, and Jerry Hicks. *The Law of Attraction: The Basics of the Teachings of Abraham.* Hay House, 2006.

Howard, Vernon. *The Esoteric Encyclopedia of Eternal Knowledge*. New Life Foundation, 1996.

Icke, David. *The Biggest Secret: The Book That Will Change the World*. 2nd updated ed., Bridge of Love Publications (UK), 1 Oct. 1998.

Isaacson, Walter. *Einstein: His Life and Universe*. Simon & Schuster, 2007.

Jamison, Harold L. "Herbalist Found Not Guilty in 'Fake' Healing Case." New York Amsterdam News, 1 Oct. 1988.

Kaku, Michio. *Hyperspace and a Theory of Everything*. Michio Kaku's Official Website, mkaku.org, 2025.

Kennedy, David O., et al. "Effects of Sage on Mood, Anxiety, and Performance in Human Volunteers." Neuropsychopharmacology, vol. 31, 2006.

Kirkpatrick, Sidney D. *Edgar Cayce: An American Prophet*. Riverhead Books, 2000.

Kramer, Samuel Noah. *The Sumerians: Their History, Culture, and Character*. University of Chicago Press, 1963.

Jefferson, Thomas. *The Life and Morals of Jesus of Nazareth*. Compiled 1820. Quoted in a letter to John Adams, 24 Jan. 1814. *Founders Online*, National Archives, https://founders.archives.gov/documents/Jefferson/03-07-02-0304.

Laszlo, Ervin. *Science and the Akashic Field: An Integral Theory of Everything*. Inner Traditions, 2004.

Marciniak, Barbara. *Bringers of the Dawn: Teachings from the Pleiadians*. Bear & Company (Inner Traditions), 1992.

"Michael Jackson's Personal Affirmations Helped Him Make Thriller the Biggest Selling Album of All Time." MichaelJackson.com, 21 Oct. 2024.

Metzger, Bruce M. *The Canon of the New Testament: Its Origin, Development, and Significance*. Oxford University Press, 1987.

Mounce, William D. *Mounce's Complete Expository Dictionary of Old and New Testament Words*. Zondervan, 2006.

Nautiyal, C. S., et al. "Medicinal Smoke Reduces Airborne Bacteria." Journal of Ethnopharmacology, vol. 114, no. 3, 2007, pp. 446–451.

Pagels, Elaine. *The Gnostic Gospels*. Random House, 1979.

Pietrzak, Robert H., et al. "Resilience in the Face of Disaster: Prevalence and Longitudinal Course of Mental Disorders Following Hurricane Ike." *PLoS ONE*, vol. 7, no. 6, 26 June 2012, e38964.

Reeves, Nicholas, and Richard H. Wilkinson. *The Complete Valley of the Kings*. Thames & Hudson, 1996.

Roberts, Jane. *Seth Speaks: The Eternal Validity of the Soul*. Prentice-Hall, 1972.

Roberts, Jane. *The Seth Material*. Bantam Books, 1984.

Roberts, Scott Alan. *The Rise and Fall of the Nephilim: The Untold Story of Fallen Angels, Giants on the Earth, and Their Extraterrestrial Origins*. Red Wheel/Weiser, 2012.

Robinson, Rich. "Ritual Washings and Baptism." Jews for Jesus, 1 Jan. 1991, www.jewsforjesus.org/blog/ritual-washings-and-baptism.

Rueckert, Carla, Don Elkins, and Jim McCarty. *The Ra Material: The Law of One*, Books 1–5. L/L Research, 1984–1998. Sessions 17.11 & 50.5. https://www.llresearch.org.

Schlauch, Karen A., et al. "Using Phenome-Wide Association Studies and the SF-12 Quality of Life Metric to Identify

Profound Consequences of ACE on Adult Mental and Physical Health in a Northern Nevadan Population." *Frontiers in Psychiatry*, 5 Oct. 2022, https://doi.org/10.3389/fpsyt.2022.984366.

Schoch, Robert M. "Redating the Great Sphinx of Giza." KMT: A Modern Journal of Ancient Egypt, vol. 3, no. 2, 1992, pp. 52–59.

Sitchin, Zecharia. *The Complete Earth Chronicles: The 12th Planet; The Stairway to Heaven; The Wars of Gods and Men; The Lost Realms; When Time Began; The Cosmic Code; The End of Days*. Bear & Company/ William Morrow, 1976–2007.

Sugrue, Thomas. *There Is a River*. ARE Press, 1997

Tanner, Norman P., editor. *Decrees of the Ecumenical Councils, Vol. 2: Trent to Vatican II.* Georgetown University Press, 1990.

Taraborrelli, J. Randy. *Michael Jackson: The Magic, The Madness, The Whole Story, 1958–2009*. Grand Central Publishing, 2009.

Tesla, Nikola. *My Inventions: The Autobiography of Nikola Tesla*. Barnes & Noble Books, 1995

Thriller 40. Directed by Nelson George, featuring Michael Jackson, Optimum Productions, 2023.

Todeschi, Kevin J. *Edgar Cayce on the Akashic Records*. ARE Press, 2010.

Unacknowledged: An Exposé of the World's Greatest Secret. Directed by Michael Mazzola, featuring Steven M. Greer, Auroris Media/Star Unacknowledged LLC, 2017.

Vermes, Geza. *The Complete Dead Sea Scrolls in English.* Penguin Classics, 1997.

von Däniken, Erich. *Chariots of the Gods? Unsolved Mysteries of the Past.* Translated by Michael Heron, Putnam, 1970.

Weiss, Brian L. *Many Lives, Many Masters: The True Story of a Prominent Psychiatrist, His Young Patient, and the Past-Life Therapy That Changed Both Their Lives.* Simon & Schuster, 1988.

Winter, Jay. *The Complete Book of Enoch: Standard English Version.* Winter Publications, 2015. TheCompleteBookOfEnochStandardEnglishVersionJayWinter

Zinn, Howard. *A People's History of the United States.* Harper Perennial Modern Classics, 2005.

Zukav, Gary. *The Dancing Wu Li Masters.* Perennial Classics, 2001.

About the Author

Sophia is a licensed therapist, holistic healer, and spiritual teacher. As a Black woman author and advocate for inclusivity in the metaphysical and alternative healing space, she brings a unique and authentic voice to spiritual literature—making ancient wisdom and esoteric teachings accessible and relatable for diverse audiences.

With a bachelor's in psychology, a master's in marriage and family therapy, along with certifications in various healing methods, her therapeutic approach is informed by both clinical practice and a lifelong journey of spiritual awakening.

From a young age, Sophia experienced vivid psychic experiences that sparked a curiosity about her soul's purpose beyond the religious traditions she had been trained to follow. She has extensively researched esoteric philosophies and traveled to various sacred sites expanding her understanding of consciousness, healing, and human evolution.

She believes that one of the most important aspects of human life is helping others awaken from the deep spiritual amnesia so many are currently experiencing. Through *Soul Walk*, Sophia offers a transformative guide that blends storytelling, spiritual wisdom, and therapeutic depth to support others in awakening to their inner truth and walking their unique soul path with intention, clarity, and courage.

www.prosperityhouse.co

www.youtube.com/@rhythmoflifetv

www.ingramcontent.com/pod-product-compliance
Lightning Source LLC
Chambersburg PA
CBHW051142120626
46547CB00012B/918